# As Long As You Need

## PERMISSION TO GRIEVE

## J.S. PARK

W PUBLISHING GROUP

AN IMPRINT OF THOMAS NELSON

ISBN 978-1-4003-3684-5 (softcover)
ISBN 978-14003-3685-2 (eBook)

**Library of Congress Control Number: 2023951447**

*Printed in the United States of America*

24 25 26 27 28 LBC 5 4 3 2 1

*For my family,*
*for my patients,*
*for my colleagues—*
*I am, for you are,*
*and I will, for we are.*

# CONTENTS

# CONTENTS

# INTRODUCTION

## Bravo, Memory, Honor

A man is wheeled into the trauma bay of the Emergency Department, and he has no memory. No identity. No history. He is charted as a series of wild happenings—a stab wound and sepsis and intractable pain. But no name.

Every patient who enters the trauma bay is given a Doe name. He is Bravo Doe. When I visit Bravo, he asks me:

"Chap—if I don't know anybody, who will grieve for me?"

I blink at him. He blinks at me. And sort of laughs. He knows I don't know how to answer.

"Can you find somebody?" he asks, laughing between blinking.

Hospital chaplains are tasked with Next-of-Kin Searches. Start with the patient's chart, filled with notes by paramedics and nurses and physicians and social workers, each document a piece of narrative, and look for fragments of names, possibly family or caretaker or surrogate. Then a public database, social media, arrest records. Call local law enforcement, other hospitals, homeless shelters. Follow a string of leads, call dozens of numbers, get a lot of wrong ones.

I get lucky once in a while. An old roommate or coworker knows a guy who knows a guy. I get the story: estranged twelve years from family, or the patient lost his house and his kids and his mind, or she fell into a gutter and nobody caught her.

Sometimes family takes the next flight over. Sometimes they tell me, "Never call here again."

But for Bravo Doe—we can't find anyone.

"What will happen to my body?" he asks. "Who takes it?"

"The county," I tell him. I hardly get the words out. "Cremation."

Cremated by the county without a trace.

"Did anything happen?" Bravo asks me.

"How do you mean?" I ask.

"If I forgot everything, did I really live?"

"Yes," I tell him. "I would like to think so."

"I'll forget you," Bravo says. "Will you remember me?"

"Yes," I say. "I will."

"It's okay if you don't. In a hundred years, none of us will. What do you think will become of us? Who will remember us? Who will tell our stories?"

I want to tell him again that I'll remember him. But I don't know that I will. I tell him, "I'd like to think God is real and God does that sort of thing."

Bravo's eyes close. He seems to recall something. "I think if God is really God, then God remembers us. Every one of us. Memory is God's love. That's a sort of love that we can't do."

Bravo leans in, holding out his hand. "Chap. You'll grieve me, right?"

I return my hand.

"Yes," I tell him. "I already do, Bravo. I will."

I tried to be with Bravo before he died. So he wouldn't be alone when it happened.

But he was alone.

Without a trace, he was gone.

What I learned from Bravo Doe is that without grief, it is impossible to impart meaning. The one thing worse than loss is for that loss to spin adrift, a footnote with no point of reference.

Grief makes it possible to connect a smear of stars into a constellation. If you can name this loss, even the nameless gain a foothold, if only for a brief moment.

I have seen hundreds of people die—but in learning their stories, I have also seen them live.

At a deathbed, with the patient hooked to a tangle of tubes and mystery bags, an early burial under plastic and bleached linens, I ask the patient's family:

"What was she like?"

They share snippets. Then stories. Adjectives turn to verbs. First full of sorrow. But almost always followed by laughter.

The fragments turn a patient into a person. The way you imagine David emerging from marble. Entropy upside-down, a valley turned mountaintop.

At the edge of memory, the dead are brought to life. Remembrance is resurrection.

I suppose this is what a chaplain does. I am a grief catcher. I catch stories. I catch bodies. I catch memories. I catch the dead. I may have never met them alive, but in my dreams I do.

In all my time with all my patients, with their families, and with the staff who love them, this is what I have learned. I have discovered a truth about grief that has broken every myth I once believed.

*Grief, it seems, is not about letting go, but about letting in.*

What I mean is, the world wants to keep spinning when you suffer loss. Let go, turn the page, move on, they say, or else the loss will consume you. If you're in it right now, you know what I mean. Your world is on fire and everybody is telling you to cool down.

And I'm telling you that the loss will consume you anyway. I'm telling you that when your world stops, you are right to pause there, to honor the whole axis and gravity and orbit of that loss.

When the grief is all you have left, it's a cruelty to lose that too.

The way I've seen it, I can tell you grief is like this.

Grief is a time transplant. It's merging, enlarging, weaving the story of all that is gone into the jagged gap of what was.

Grief is not acceptance. It is defiance and rebellion. The body knows this loss is irreparable, irreplaceable. Really, the body knows it is almost wrong. Because even when we try to forget, our bodies have a way of surfacing memory through the pores.

Grief is the debt we pay to live and to love and to chase the stuff that gives us meaning. Every breath is a debt collection on a collapsing hallway of deficit. You are a life on loan.

Grief is your own. The DNA of your grief is universal in its humanity but specifically yours in its expression.

Grief is lament. It is outrage at all the ways that life is taken. Somebody is randomly swallowed up by the earth, or swept into the poisoned river of systemic failure, or snatched by evil hands—this sort of grief is lifelong agony, and it lives in the stomach.

Grief is the voice of what is gone. Not only the people we lose, but dreams unmade, dignity frayed, pictures with emptied frames.

You can try to bury that sort of thing. I get it. I've tried it. Seems a lot easier to sever or jettison it, or shove it all into a box and force it shut. But the more you try to bury grief, the more it demands to be heard. The more you deny what the loss meant to you, the more you disappear yourself. The voice of grief makes its way through the seams, bursting at every clasp. The voice of everyone and everything buried runs up your throat, demanding to shout itself into being again.

Grief is a story gasping to be told.

I'm telling you this because nobody else told me:

*There is no such thing as closure.*

There is no final stitch, no last loop.

We do not move on. We move with.[1]

The thing is, a lot of our ideas about grief are inherited from unhealthy survival mechanisms. We've attempted to delete the pain in the hard drive and overwrite it with a rushed and quiet compliancy. The latest update of the *DSM*, the *Diagnostic and Statistical Manual of Mental Disorders*,[2] says that "prolonged grief disorder" is grief that lasts longer than six months for children and teens, and longer than a year for adults.[3] Apparently, on day 366 of your grief, you have a "disorder."

I get it. Numbers are clean and appealing. I would prefer to solve the grief neatly myself if I could. Wouldn't you? I would prefer a sequentially ordered manual of metrics to the brutal work of walking through a world on fire. The typical formula for grief emerges from a controlled lab, a carefully crafted progression of

$X$, one teardrop at the edge of one eyeball plus one lip tremble minus any yelling or throwing of chairs,

plus $Y$, a movie montage of swelling violin and casseroles and spin class multiplied by taking a shower divided by dating a new lover,

equals $Z$, a final scene of flowers on a grave and turning the page to a colorful springtime summit where you reach the end credits and every credit is you.

You have twelve months to accomplish this. Or half that if you're a child. Preferably less.

But no human is solved by math. So the first thing I recommend, really, is to throw this book across the room. Or the chair. Don't calculate the arc or velocity. Let it fly. And your tears too.

Then, if you decide to stop reading this book right here, that's okay. If you're grieving, I get it. If I were you, I wouldn't want to read a book like this either.

If you keep going, I hope I can impart three things.

One: Your loss is yours and nobody else's.

Two: Your loss is not something you get over, but something you carry everywhere you go.

And three: You can take as long as it takes.

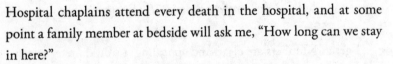

Hospital chaplains attend every death in the hospital, and at some point a family member at bedside will ask me, "How long can we stay in here?"

The nurses and physicians and chaplain all have the same answer.

"Take as long as you need."

Does the body have to go soon? Yes.

Does the room need to be cleared soon? Yes.

Do the staff have to leave eventually? Yes.

But will we ever rush you out of there? No.

Everybody gets their time. That time is your grief.

I am a hospital chaplain, which means I see the dead and dying around the clock.

Maybe you're not sure what a hospital chaplain is. After eight years of wearing a chaplain badge, I wish they'd tell me too. But my usual reply is that I'm a cross between a priest and a therapist. I'm a thera-priest.

Every time I've sat with loss, I've gained something too. It's never a thing I wanted, but it's a thing that helped me survive. I don't mean to say that loss teaches you a lesson or that it's God's Will or something. But I want to tell you about how grief gave me itself. Everybody else rushed me past the agony, but grief is the one and only voice that told me: *Take as long as you need.*

*Part One*

# LOSING SPIRIT

*one*

# LOSS OF FUTURE DREAMS: A SKIP IN TIME

## On intrapsychic grief: the pain of losing what will never be

Content warning: This chapter contains descriptions of end-of-life care, vehicular collision, and assault. Reader, please be advised.

*The memory is the entire. The longing in the face of the lost. Maintains the missing. Fixed between the wax and wane indefinite not a sign of progress. All else age, in time. Except. Some are without.*

—THERESA HAK KYUNG CHA, *DICTEE*[1]

"You made it," my patient says, and she calls me by her son's name. Her son died years ago. Overdose. Alleyway. Found days later.

"You found me," my patient says. Her eyes brim red. "You're here," she says.

I open my mouth to correct her. To tell her I'm the chaplain. Not her son. And I pause on my intake of breath. How do I answer? Should

I lie? Should I tell her the truth? A child dying like that, maybe it's better to forget.

One school of thought says you correct the patient, reaffirm reality no matter how hard that might be, or else you risk feeding a delusion and setting your patient up for a big crash down the line. Another school of thought says you aren't there to correct a patient, but to be a companion in their condition. That while it might go wrong later, the right thing is to focus on what the patient needs in this moment.

She stretches her hand out to me.

I open my mouth again.

I want to tell you why I answered the way I did.

I hope you won't be too hard on me. How I see grief, how I enter grief: The hospital has changed all of that. Patients, families, staff all enter with a life lined up and exit with a life sideways. The hospital. It's the one place you enter the front but come out the side.

## A PAPER FUTURE, FOLDED AND FRAYED

What I see most in the hospital is not just death and dying, but the death of dreams.

If you've ever suffered loss, you know what I mean. Around every loss, there radiates an overwhelming wave of decimation. If the past is a distant and receding island, the future is a sinking and opaque horizon.

Every patient I see, they're bursting with the life they'll never get to live.

**Patient 1:** She types on her phone's notepad that she misses singing. Her throat cancer is back. It's also the four-year anniversary of her daughter's death. She used to sing to her daughter during her chemo treatments.

**Patient 2**: Her fiancé hasn't visited since the accident. She knows it's over.

**Patient 3**: He will never walk again. He had gone out for a midnight snack with his best friend. He will miss his best friend's funeral. His best friend was the driver.

**Patient 4**: Code Blue. Forty-four minutes into resuscitation. The new liver was supposed to work. His wife asks me to pray. In the middle of the prayer, they call it: "Time of death, 1307."

**Patient 5**: She lost her child at sixteen weeks. Her son lived for seven hours. She asks me, "How do you grieve someone you never met?"

With each patient, I hear similar questions. It keeps emerging, this pulse. It presses in every room, leans on every shoulder, demands an answer: *How do you grieve future loss?* Underneath that, more questions: *How do you deal with the viciousness of a broken dream? How do you move on from the picture of life in your head? How do you keep moving through a parallel-universe life?*

My patients suffer from good dreams. What I mean is, it's not the nightmares that keep them up. It's the hope. Daydreams of another life. Instead of homesick, they're timesick.

Before becoming a chaplain, I thought grief was about missing the past. About reflecting on all the things before, the stuff we had until mortality crawled through the window. It's true. We grieve the past. But mostly no one gets a chance to grieve the future. It doesn't seem to read as a real loss.

I need to tell you about this because nobody told me:

*The dream that didn't happen is as much of a loss as losing the one that did.*

# THREE SECONDS FOR THE REST OF YOUR LIFE

I visit Zaniah. She closes her eyes and tells me about another life—the *before* life. Before the bilateral amputation, thirty percent TBSA (total body surface area) burn, and before the hospital bed became her second world. Before the before-and-after.

"Try to imagine," Zaniah says in fits and starts, her TBI (traumatic brain injury) stealing her speech. "You take three extra seconds on your way." In that delay, the universe opens up an abyss beneath her, fast as a thunderclap. She becomes *automobile versus pedestrian*, or what the Emergency Department will abbreviate to *Auto vs. Ped*. She's on the sidewalk. Then pinned by the vehicle. There is an explosion. "You wake up to be told that your brain has been sheared in multiple places by the force of the collision. Your legs had to be amputated to save your life. They say you're lucky. You remember none of it. Maybe that's the lucky part."

She tells me to sit with those three seconds—you dropped your phone or took another sip of coffee or waved to a new face—and you are now in a branched timeline leading you to this hospital bed.

What if you had not taken those three seconds? Things would have resumed as normal.

But with that small skip in time.

The film judders.

And now you are here.

You will question those three seconds for the rest of your life. Angry or ashamed or resigned. It's enough to keep you up. Not with nightmares, I don't think. But awake with good dreams. Good enough to hurt.

She tells me, "I miss it, you know. I miss the things that were supposed to be."

I open my mouth to say something. I breathe in. Pause my tongue. Bite my breath. What is there to say, really? What do you tell a person who grieves their future? How do you say, "I'm sorry for your future loss"?

When I visit a patient, I enter their other timeline. At the edge of bedside is their eroded vision of a life that was supposed-to-be. They step off that bed and they're stepping into a chasm of the irretrievable. A not-yet that never-will. I hear scraps and fragments, endings of beginnings:

> "—got fourth place, and that's the last time I can try, I completely—"
>
> "—fell apart, I was one more unlucky guy in the pandemic, I was supposed to—"
>
> "—have dinner next week with her before the heart attack, I had to—"
>
> "—say those words, I wish I could've just told him what he meant to me but—"
>
> "—I regretted it the second I said it, the look on my son's face, I should've—"
>
> "—left but I stayed, hoping it would get better, I wasted thirty-five years with him, I—"
>
> "—look back all the time, and I wonder *what now?*"

It wasn't until I sat with patient after patient, from emergency room to deathbed, that I saw what they saw: In their illness or injury, I saw a *memory loss of the future.* This is called *intrapsychic grief,* the pain of losing what will never be, the reaching for something that was supposed to happen.

This intrapsychic grief is a specific but universal ache. One of my fellow chaplains put it like this: "When she lost her friend, it wasn't just the loss of relational history, secrets kept, inside jokes, but the loss of a dinner appointment the next week, milestones down the road, the promise of more."

I didn't know how to grieve that sort of loss, for me or my patients. How do you honor that sort of thing? The loss of a memory unmade?

Amid this sort of grief, I noticed two things my patients and I had to get through:

a *lie* about how we hold our losses

and a *dilemma* in choosing how we let them go.

Like everything else with grief, none of it was what I expected.

## ONE MORE TIME, I WOULD

But first, I need to tell you about one of my earliest patient encounters. I learned real fast then how little I knew about grief, how we have learned to say things around death that only squeeze the room out of a room.

They wheel him in and we know it's too late. The only thing left is for his mother to decide on his organs. He's young, good-looking, face marked by meth. You've heard this story a thousand times. It's a tragedy a thousand times. His mother had given him a free bed and third chances, an open door and warm breakfasts, but he relapsed on replay. His mom finally kicked him out. And he didn't fight, she said. His last words were, "I get it, Mom. I'm too much." Her son found an abandoned tenement to soothe himself. Then he took too much. Someone called an ambulance. He was found alone.

The brain test revealed brain death. The only thing the hospital could do was keep him breathing. His bed was a mess of tentacles, sprouting and twisting in veiny circles. Past the machines, I could see he was a kid. Just a kid. Just an addict. Just a patient. Just a future.

"Just one more time," his mom says. "I could've let him stay. He wasn't getting better. I mean, what could I do? I couldn't do it anymore. His eyes were gone. He was already gone. But I could've tried one more time."

We bring her up to the ICU. She sees her son and she folds in half. Briefly I look away. It's too much to bear. To see the love of a mother who has to say goodbye to her baby boy.

She strokes his chest as it rises and falls on the tide of the ventilator. She weeps over his tubes and his arms. She finally grabs his face and says, "Sorry, I'm sorry. I would one more time. I would." She thought she was doing the right thing. How could she have known?

The rest of the family trickles in. We sit them down and go over a form that could possibly cover his hospital expenses. I hate this part. The form asks, "Was he in college? Was he working? Was he in the military?" His mother says softly, "No. No. No." A page full of unchecked boxes. She burrows into her seat.

She tells me about every dream she prayed over her womb to every extended hand for her prodigal to come home and every part of me wants to scream her son awake and unbury his body from its grave of tubes and IVs and machines and reach back into *one more time*.

After eleven hours, his mother decides.

"Unplug it." She points to the machines, then to her son. "Use every organ. It's okay. I'm okay."

The family, one by one, say their goodbyes. One more time. We pray. And the mother says to her son, "You're finally free."

If I could go back there, I'd change my approach. That form with the checkboxes? I would've torn it up. Saved it for another time. Once in a while a form like this is helpful in the room; some families need anything to sign, to do, to decide. But not this time. I misread the room, badly. My patient's mother didn't need a visual of unchecked boxes. That was no way to honor her son, to disgrace him in his last breath. If you ask me, nobody should be measured against a checklist like that.

What I came to understand is that I was only reminding my patient's mother that her son had died. A life cut short, and somehow also a life that didn't fulfill a rigid and imposed outline of value. I wish I would've paused. Paused for the dignity due beyond the boxes. Given some room to grieve a mother's dream. The dream of her son. To talk about what was, to say what could've been. I rushed past to get to some functional form—a helpful one, I think, but part of the relentless march forward to forget.

Part of grief, I have found, is to look at the things that are not and to give some language to them. To bust open the box and make some breathing room. I was too quick to pull the sheet over their losses.

## THE LIE: LET GO OF GRIEF AND YOU HEAL FASTER

I would keep hearing the same lie that I first pushed on a family for checkboxes on a form—not pausing, but pulling their heels past their feelings even as their fingernails clawed concrete—this lie piercing through every hospital bed, coiling around hearts and guts. It was a lie I believed and perpetuated. You've seen this lie in motion. The lie that grief is a sort of poisonous shame that must be removed by force.

The lie that looks like:

Patients beating their own chests to stuff down their tears.

Family embarrassed for crying too hard over the body of their loved one.

Family and clergy and sometimes staff telling the patient to look past it, get over it, don't worry about it—anything but look right at it.

And the lie sounds like those one-liners. You know the kind:

It's just God's Will.

It was meant to be.

Heaven just got another angel.

It gets better.

Look on the bright side.

Everything happens for a reason.

Everything has a purpose.

At least it makes you stronger.

At least you have—

At least at least at least at least.

The thing I kept hearing was to *let go and start again*. Get some new dreams down the street, I guess. People start over every day, they say. Heal faster, why don't you?

This is a very attractive lie. At first glance, it's almost a noble one. It's hard to stay in pain. It's hard to see somebody in pain. So the urge to fix pain is understandable. It's born of charity, our innate need to make right and to rescue. Survival becomes a way of forcefully turning your neck to look away from grief. It's as if grief is some toxic contagious substance that everybody has to bury as quick as their dead. We attempt to rush into solution and conclusion and hope—because pain is that hard.

The lie of *Letting Go* is powered by a simple and harmful myth: that when we hold our losses closely, somehow we do ourselves more harm. And if you suffer an "invisible loss"—the death of a dream, the loss of a future, the collapse of something that hasn't happened yet—this gets even less dignity than the deceased does. If the loss of a whole person is already so suppressed, then the loss of a dream never stood a chance.

I've seen how harmful it gets when we try to move on so quickly. There is a sprinting to closure, not just with platitudes and bad theology, but by the urgent demand to get you back to top shape, to work mode, to the hustle and grind, to happy smiles—all to quell everyone else's own sense of inconvenience.

I visit Zaniah, my patient with burns, again. The nurse tells me before I enter the room, "Her family's bedside. And her *pastor too*." The way the nurse says "pastor too" turns my spine funny.

I enter and there stands her pastor. He looks at me, then my hair, then my shoes, back to my hair. He says, "They make baby chaplains now, huh?"

"Yep," I tell the pastor. "They popped me right out of seminary."

At that, the room busts up. One of them even roars laughter from his stomach. I laugh too. I can't help myself. Hearing laughter in a hospital room is always a gift, a hint of green in a desert.

But the pastor gives me a look, draws back his lips until they're razors. I get that stare as if I'm a stain he has to bleach. I try to feel bad. I really try. I almost make it.

I introduce myself. Zaniah smiles, which I can tell hurts her a bit, and she says, "I'm glad you're here. Would you please pray for me?" Her pastor twitches like he quietly slipped a disc. So Zaniah adds, "We could always use more prayer."

Her family, about a dozen people, gather in a circle, standing room only. I'm directly next to her on her right side. The pastor squeezes in to my left, almost between me and the bed. He has a smell. I can't pinpoint it, but my guess is starched plaid shirt and years of institutional decay.

As always, I ask my patient, "What's the biggest thing I can pray about for you right now?"

I hear a cough. The pastor says, "For God to do a miracle, what else?" He coughs again, on my neck.

Zaniah begins to weep. She says, "This surgery. It's risky. I don't know how to . . . I don't know."

"No no no, don't worry," the pastor chimes in. He chimes real hard. "You trust God, you don't have to cry, you don't worry. Just hush now."

For a moment Zaniah was about to say more—that extra bit of release and relief to unearth all that's been buried—but she closes her mouth and nods at her pastor. I notice the way her breath draws in, her words bit between teeth, the fear thrown back in her throat. Just the briefest breath: I've seen it dozens of times, the way we adjust ourselves out of embarrassment or conformity or the dread that we'll be seen as a *burden*, an emotional liability; *it's already so much that I'm sick, I don't want to add more to my family.*

I know I've inadvertently gotten ahead of my patients, too, when I was too eager to pitch in and solve, and they pull back, try to reply to my reply, to keep me there, to hold my interest as if they owe me for being in need. I always try to go back, but that holy moment of disclosure evaporates as quick as it appears. Sometimes in half a second, the fastest flinch, I see a rift open and there's a galaxy of stories swirling under the skin, and then it's gone. These moments can't easily be scheduled or re-created. Vulnerability is a shooting star, I think, a child who knocks on your door at three in the morning, holding a hard question, afraid, not that you don't have answers but that you won't answer. You get a handful of those moments before those hands close up for good.

I lean closer. I tell Zaniah, "It sounds scary."

She lets out the breath she has taken. "It is," she says in that breath. "It is." She almost says she's scared, but she grips that in the air between us.

Her pastor turns his head to me. I glance at him and he is flexing the most severe, sour look I've ever seen. I imagine this is his idea of God, who looks at him the same way.

I start to pray. Halfway through my prayer, I feel something to my left. It feels like the wheel of the bed is slowly rolling onto my left foot. I take a look. I try not to gasp. No kidding, this pastor is stepping on my foot, forcing his right leg in front of my left leg, pressing his hip over mine, creeping over like an inchworm. Pushing me back. Our legs make the most unfortunate pretzel. His right shoulder ends up in my jaw. I'm almost sure he's grinning to himself.

He keeps inching. I keep praying.

This cliché-dealing pastor is like a panicked time traveler. But instead of going back in time to fix something, he is trying to take everybody forward with him to skip the pain and cut straight to the promised land—even if that means dislocating elbows, skinning shins, tearing hair, pulling us all to some hopeful heaven where nobody has to go through the hard part. Maybe he doesn't want to admit, just like I didn't in the beginning, that the hard part is the whole thing.

I try to find him later. I want some sort of catharsis or connection, that look of understanding between two colleagues. I make up a whole story in my head about his past, his hurts, his silence, his lonely nights in the study, his terror at the pulpit, his inability to address his depression or performance pressure because he believes that would disqualify him from ministry.

I imagine this other timeline where, after my visit, I see the pastor in the hallway and I say to him, "I know this is hard. How are you holding up?" And that gets him to open up. Maybe he tells me,

*"I'm sorry about the weird leg thing. I'm defensive right now because I feel threatened by the possibility you'll cause my church members to stumble and to undo all the three-point sermons I've been sweating over at the pulpit and I'm uncomfortable in the face of suffering that forces me to confront my own beliefs about the goodness of God, and look, if I don't trust God—that is, perfectly recite the doctrine I've been questioning so I can prop up my doctrinal creed—then what does that say about me as a pastor, especially when the offering plate goes around? Also, the smell of rubbing alcohol reminds me of my mother who was on life support for three weeks and God never answered my prayer."*

Maybe I can tell him that I get it, that sometimes this social pressure to appear *theologically sound* gets us saying strange stuff that's not about our parishioners or patients, but that's really about our own subterranean river of the unexamined. I wish I could dig deep with that pastor, turn back the wheel-lock on that vault together, figure out why theology has become this weaponized standard of proof instead of a ballast in a churning ocean.

If I could just find him, I know we'll get to the montage of high-fiving and staring cooperatively out a window. Maybe something new clicks in him and he tells our patient and parishioner, "I see you are scared and I am here." I picture us teaming up, taking turns, praying in circles, clergy duo, crosses in hand, communion wafers up on three, let's lay down every scrap of pretension and just weep with our people.

I find him. In the hallway. I'm about to say something. He bends down from his great height and speaks first. He says four words. Just these four:

"Now's not the time."

I want to smile. Sure, we're professionals here. But I get out of character. I ask a question. Also four words.

"When is it ever?"

For a second, his eyebrows do a thing. Maybe remorse. Maybe disgust. He turns on his heel and presses the elevator button.

No catharsis. I watch that timeline vanish down the elevator.

## THE DILEMMA: I HAVE TO FIX THIS

Really, that pastor probably had a piece of the right idea: Let's forget the future you lost and try to focus on some hopeful future you can have.

I get that. When somebody you love is in pain, you feel a particular desperation, a frustration. I'm sure you've felt it, up against the glass bubble of someone else's tragedy, impermeable. You want to help but you warble off-key, you stab at eloquent words, you try a phrase and it only clangs. It's a helpless feeling. Especially for a caregiver type who carries compassion so deep it's always at critical mass and from it there explodes a frantic search for a box of tissues or ice water or a warm blanket or wise quotes or a referral to this therapist or a book or a group or a million other actionable ideas, because you want to make this the turning point. You care. You care enough to take their agony.

There has to be some perfect combination of words to set this person up for a successful upward journey through grief—and we clutch that thought because it hurts to see people hurt. In my early days, I overreached with resources and ideas and four-course meals. I'd see families writhing on the floor, and I'd hover as long as I could and I'd probably overstay, until it was too awkward to leave. Some just needed three minutes of listening, or a thirty-second prayer.

In those early patient visits, I knew I was missing something. Sometimes I still am. I believed the lie of letting go so strongly that I just wanted to help patients surrender their grief. I had to have answers, to be the answer, I couldn't stand to see someone wounded, so I'd pick them up as fast as I could, even if the edges of fractured bones scraped and grated. I lacked some fundamental component of listening, understanding, tuning in. I attempted to be some elevating positive inspirational force, but I knew by the shut-down looks on my patients' faces that I was beyond the language of grief, outside the wavelength, the wound.

I know that's how it goes sometimes. We can't hope to connect with everyone all the time. But I was stumbling badly, as if chasing after trains that had departed with my patient inside. I was always a second behind the connection, my thumbs jabbing between the sliding doors to pry them open and jump on, but they were gone. I felt I was on the verge of comprehending some elusive truth close enough to reach, but then I'd grab the wind.

A nurse told me once, "He just stood there over his wife. Fifty years together and she's gone. What can I do? Give him food, a ride, hotel voucher, autopsy, a prayer. What else can I do? Feels helpless. I don't mean to make it about me. But it's like—there's this itch, I have to fix this. And I can't. Tomorrow, I'm back here. To do what I can when I can't."

What I've found is that people who throw clichés and one-liners at sickness are not always malicious; they're saying those things to soothe everybody, including themselves. It's an evacuation from despair. When suffering is so overwhelming that it approaches the Cliffs of Uncertainty Where Anything Bad Can Happen, I've seen how anyone, me included, can attempt to insert future hope into present loss. It's a way to cope. I get that. And maybe it works once in a while.

But the problem is that a future is not so easily buried. To rush forward in time, pulling this eschatological curtain over our losses so we don't have to look over the cliff that would unravel all the certainty we've built up about God or the universe or the way things are supposed to work out—I mean, I know, who wants to look there anyway? We rush past the abyss because it's rushing toward us all. We grab these clichés because we think they're branches on the way down, but they turn out to be cobwebs. So instead of honoring memory, we build up the muscle of denial.

In most rooms now, I'm a ruinous presence. No eschatological curtains allowed, but a real look over the cliff's edge. I can't sweeten suffering. I can't sweep it under a veil. But I can look the loss in the eyes.

## THE GHOST OF PAST PASSED

I've found that those spinning in future loss are torn between two timelines: the *original one* they were supposed to be in, and then *this one*, the one they aren't. They're being told to move past that other future, the one they wanted, to start living in this one, the one they don't. Just cut clean and cauterize, it's gone, make the most of what you've got now, make a new castle out of these glass shards. I've seen this sort of thing a thousand times. No doubt I've been guilty of it. The urge to rush pain forward in time. You're expected to get back on schedule. Get your stuff in order. Make the arrangements. Take the shower. Only in loss, your world has stopped. Time has stopped.

There is a short story by author Ted Chiang called "Anxiety Is the Dizziness of Freedom" in which a device called a prism can show a parallel universe. There are recovery groups for those addicted to viewing their parallel lives. The story follows a married couple who gets into an accident, and in one universe, one half of the couple survives. In another universe, the other half of the couple survives. The surviving halves of the couple find the exact prisms they need to talk with each other. The prism has a limited amount of usage, but because the accident was sudden, the couple can use that extra bit of time to say goodbye.[2] This is never presented as an addiction or dysfunction, but something this couple needs to be able to go on. Maybe this is what we need too: memory refracted by a prism to cherish all its color.

Speeding through grief always has a cost. To bury somebody's supposed-to-be is also to bury a story that's untold. When you bury someone's story like that, it gets lodged in the ribcage, it gets radioactive, it festers, it shouts to be heard. *Grief is always a voice that needs to speak.* If you suppress it, it still speaks—but not always in ways that are healthy. Not in the ways you need. It pushes through your skin like rogue splinters.

Burying a future loss without telling its story can make you sick. Timesick. You get split between timelines. The further along you go, the further away you get from that dream, and you look around and wonder how people can keep going while you want the world to stop, time to freeze, to get back to your real universe. And you get well-meaning people around you, always the ones who mean well, who are nudging you forward, shoving you, really, and you clutch two timelines until you're ripped in half.

Part of my role as a chaplain, I've learned, is to make room for these original timelines. That they may be spoken, shared. The story told. "There is no agony like bearing an untold story inside you," Zora Neale Hurston said.[3] It must be conversely true that there is no greater peace than to tell that story. It is the very voice of that telling that moves us into being whole again.

# I DREAM TO SURVIVE

청천하늘엔 잔별도 많고,
우리네 가슴엔 희망도 많다.

*Just as many faint stars reside in a clear sky,
there are also as many dreams living in our hearts.*

— VERSE FROM "ARIRANG," OR "MY BELOVED
ONE," A KOREAN FOLK SONG

My patient Tony tells me he had gotten weaker and weaker in his legs until one day, on the way home, he collapsed at the ATM. Floating heads surrounded him asking what was wrong, but they looked like demon faces and he tried to kick them off, except his legs didn't move. Tony had brain lesions caused by encephalopathy.

"But you know, chap," he says, breaking into tears, "I got this long-lost brother Mikey up in Boston. He's my half-brother but he loves me like a full one—this guy's made of money and he offered me a room at his place, his house is on this fifty-acre property, it's a mansion. Can you believe it?"

I speak with Tony's sister, who tells me this brother in Boston doesn't exist. No mansion, no fifty acres. It's a story that Tony told himself when his legs began failing him. A story to hold him up.

The neurologist Oliver Sacks writes about patients who "confabulate."[4] They conjure up yarns about meeting celebrities or devising inventions or discovering something big, as if the widening chasms in their brain need these tales to thrive. One story after another keeps their brain from tumbling over the cliff. I might be the last guy to hear these tales.

Some argue that holding room for them only enables delusions. I don't disagree. Placebos work because they are the medicine of hope. Who am I to revoke a fiction made canon?

My patient Jerome has a trapezoid-shaped hole in his head. He tells me it's from his son. Jerome's son had waited in his father's home until he came back from work. Jerome's son robbed him. Amid the struggle, his son had picked up one of those bright and shiny decorative geode rocks the size of a torso, lifted it to the sky, and brought it down on his father's head. The son is still at large. After six months in physical therapy, Jerome still couldn't get the bloodstain out of the carpet. He had lost his job; his wife had left him. Jerome's other son took two jobs to pay off the hospital bills, but one evening after dropping off his dad for PT, this other son was killed by a hydroplaning eighteen-wheeler.

"Chaplain, I had this dream," Jerome says, scratching his wound, "that in another world, I was someone else. I was someone better. I have two sons who love me. My wife never left. I am still with my boys. I had a dream I was someone not me. It was extraordinary. It was wo—"

He falls asleep, which he told me would happen. His brain has to shut down when it overworks itself. A few seconds later, he wakes up and apologizes.

"I had this dream, chaplain. Do you ever dream that you are someone in another world, a different you?"

Jerome nods off again, but his eyes flutter, his mouth opens, he speaks. His voice is thicker, slower. He sits up taller. I take a step back.

Jerome's eyes quiver. He says in this new voice, "I am the man from the other world." He smiles, just for a second. "I am the man in the dream. The dream wishes he could be the man in the other. We all wish to be awake in someone else. There is no—"

He drifts, then wakes up again. I'm not sure if I should tell him about the other voice.

He says, "Chaplain, thank you." His eyes are wet, alive. "Thank you for listening. I have to believe my son didn't mean it. I still love my son, in this world or the next."

I leave the room shaking. I repeat his words. I replay the twitch of his eyes, the way his body slipped into another skin, another dimension.

I glance through a keyhole into other possibilities, where a son did not ruin his father, where a car missed by inches, where a promised land of endless acres waited at the other end. At every turn, every choice, we die a million deaths each day. How can we stand such a thing, except to tell the stories that never had a shot?

When a dream is buried, it doesn't stay under. Every dream, with its vision and possibility and fear and anticipation, stays vibrating, animated, eager to be seen in the world.

There is this condition called Charles Bonnet syndrome in which someone with vision loss begins to hallucinate in order to fill in the gaps in their sight. It is not caused by medications, mental health issues, or neurological issues. It's a function of the brain. Some see waterfalls, bugs in their food, dragons through the window, or the deceased in the living room. Our brains essentially sew patchwork for what is missing.

We survive the nightmare of loss, I think, by dreaming. To dream is to cope. It is the brain's essential defense against itself. We create new dreams all the time, a canvas of assurances against the intolerable. The world continues to be cruel and unfair, but we dream amid the wreckage of what no longer is.

That's part of my role. To honor the burial of what can never be done. To remember what will never become.

## KEEPING THE LOST WITHOUT LOSING MYSELF

How do we keep alive the memory of what was lost without denying the reality of that loss? In other words, if I keep giving voice to what was lost, am I enabling a delusion, getting stuck in daydreams, losing myself to a dead timeline? Was I enabling a fantasy by making room for my patients to echo their losses? If I am never to sweeten suffering with false hope, is it a mistake to keep dreams alive, memory alive, a parallel universe in view?

Here, I can only believe in two opposite truths at once.

*Dreams are always dying. They're tenuous. Reality drops in.*

*But dreams also keep us going. We dream again to survive.*

It's here I found this valuable gift in the middle of grieving: If somebody needs to go to the past to remember something good, that's where I go. If they need a bit of future down the road, I'm going there too. And if they need to stay in the present, even in a terrible loop of their very worst pain, that's where I stay. Without turning away.

When grief takes us time traveling, dream traveling, and hurls us into a sudden memory, it might seem dangerous, even unwanted. But I have found I can trust this grief to tell us what our body needs. Mostly, it is our body trying to rest inside the dream. Not to deny our loss, but to survive it, to honor it, to find resolve to keep dreaming.

So when my patient reveals something, even when it seems random, I assume it's for a reason. That reason is often their body seeking a meaningful tether, between the world and their dream, as if to steady themselves by a single grip in a directionless sea. This may seem basic, I suppose, but if my patient brings up a dream or childhood memory or accomplishment or trivia or favorite song, I pay attention. Most of the time, these are important disclosures that reveal an almost imperceptible need. The heart is trying to speak what the mouth cannot say. If we listen, there is always a story, and its own telling becomes medicine.[5]

In loss, after crisis, in those interminable stretches you cannot move, your mind wanders, you race to one island of thought or another. You may have heard these called intrusive or compulsive or obsessive thoughts. Something bad, we're told. But I wonder if at times a thought like that is the body sending a signal. Telling you what it needs, where it has to go, *when* it has to go.

My patient says this about a book she's reading, "My favorite part is when he went on the retreat." At the end of the visit, I call back to her words: "I know the hospital is not the retreat you wanted." And right then, she weeps.

A future that falls midflight still needs to land. An unfinished dream still looks for a way into the waking world. The world may force you to move on. But that grief story still needs to be voiced, told.

If you're able to voice this grief in some way, whether continually in small moments or with a single grand gesture, I hope you will. I hope someone will go there and then with you. Losing a dream is a death. It must be grieved. And grief needs to be spoken. Sometimes it needs to be screamed.

My patient with dementia, the one whose son died of an overdose years ago, blinks at me.

She's waiting for my reply. I have to make a choice. Do I tell her I'm the chaplain, or do I tell her I'm her son, the one she's been looking for, the one she thinks I am?

I pause too long. My patient blinks a few more times and sighs. "You're not him?"

"I'm sorry," I tell her. "I'm the—"

—*chaplain?*

What does that mean, anyway? I'm the guy between the medicine and machines. Intersection of faith and mental health. I'm a pastor but not really. I'm a counselor but not really. I'm a grief midwife or grief surgeon or grief doula. I give permission for emotions. I travel with my patient into their reality, the thing they don't want to see. Into their devastation. But also into their hopes. Into their dreams. Their worst day in that bed. Their best day before that room. I am a prism reflecting past and future, I am presence, in the present, I am a brief sounding board, flicker of light, momentary dance partner, supposedly an encourager, but also harbinger of bad news, hopefully a reminder of something bigger than ourselves, but also how fast it all goes. I am archivist, witness, historian of a history that will never happen. I am the last one to know where you wanted to be.

The lie we tell is that grief will burn us, so grief itself must be incinerated.

But in grief, there is another form of lying—not exactly a lie, but not exactly the truth.

*I had this dream, chaplain. Do you ever dream that you are someone in another world, a different you?*

I am a chaplain, and that means I dream with you. It means I dream too.

"I'm sorry," I say again. "I'm sorry I'm late."

My patient holds my hand. "I knew. I knew. They said you wouldn't come. But I knew you'd be here."

"I . . . I'm here, Mom. I'm here."

Later that night, I'm told she has died. In her sleep. Holding her own hands together. As peacefully as somebody can go.

I hope you will understand. I hope you will not be too hard on me.

*two*

# LOSS OF FAITH: A HOLE-SHAPED GOD

## On losing our worldview to suffering, and what comes after

Content warning: This chapter contains descriptions of traumatic loss, including distressing healthcare situations and infant loss. Reader, please be advised.

*Are the dead a live audience for your miracles?*
*Do ghosts ever join the choirs that praise you?*

—PSALM 88:10, MSG

I'm seeing too much.

Seven months in, I draw up my resignation letter. To quit my chaplain residency.

I had thought I knew a thing or two when I began at the hospital, centuries ago, a new chaplain with a bloated head full of big ideas. Then one by one, from stretcher to surgery, those ideas burst. Not quietly. The hospital makes sure of it. As ruthlessly as my patients' dreams had ended, so does my paper faith.

By the fourth month, I have this case I can't get out of my head. The night is rainy and hot; a man shoots his wife and his daughter, then takes his own life. The wife doesn't make it. The daughter does. I try to support her. She only asks, "What does it even mean that I 'made it'?"

That night, soaked by the rain, I pick up some inspirational book from my bookcase. I get through two sentences and I slam it shut. Thunder roars, like God is grunting. I go through a few more books. Words that might have comforted me just months ago feel crass and trivial. I'm looking for these authors' shorn edges. That's the part I want to see. Not their neat bows. I don't want a world seemingly bereft of the fallout from a future that has imploded. I need an aftermath theology. Something for the alley, for the trench. What is it like to survive shrapnel? *What does it mean to "make it"?*

Over and over, I'm in the waiting room when the doctor breaks the worst-case scenario:

*Your wife will die from the brain bleed.*

*The liver will fail.*

*The transplant isn't coming.*

*The sepsis has gone too far.*

*He will never wake up.*

*She is dead.*

I'm seeing babies born to die, abusers walking free, unthinkable pain from cancer.

I'm seeing spouses die at thirty, teens terminally extubated, resuscitations fail.

The pagers, the machines buzzing, the phones ringing—I begin to hear these in the quiet. Phantom hospital beeps. Your phone is no different: bad news cycle, always buzzing, one headline then another, midnight Amber Alerts, suspicious activity on campus. I'm told this can become alarm fatigue when the alerts are so normal you stop responding to them. I never get to alarm fatigue. Every page and phone call and occlusion alarm spikes my adrenaline. My nerves are electric eels. My arteries fill with gasoline.

The fifth month. I wake up from a nightmare with a knife pain in my left rib. Screaming does nothing. The pain is so severe I'm sure I'm bleeding. My doctor says it's a peptic ulcer.

"So, you're bleeding. No more acidic foods, no more coffee, no more stress. What do you do for work?"

"I catch bodies. I catch the dead. I make space so the grieving can vent and weep and throw things."

"That's poetic. And awful. How many do you see?"

"Hundreds. I have seen hundreds of dead and dying people and the bereaved."

"Oh." He looks up at me. "Seeing pain is causing pain. On the nose, isn't it? Here's a proton pump inhibitor. Unlimited refills."

The sixth month, I have a series of tiny panic attacks. The beeping, the bleeding, my bookcase, the dead—these converge into heart palpitations, dyspnea, Takotsubo cardiomyopathy. I'm having nightmares of my wife calling out to me from the end of a tunnel. I collapse at the hospital. I crawl to the Emergency Department between blackouts. Orthostatic hypotension. The doctor tells me I need to stand up slower and to eat more salt and to rest. She asks when I last ate. I can't remember. Not just my meal. The entire week. I only remember the names of my patients that day.

I begin to hear the dead. In hallways, in my sleep, in my backseat. I run to the end of a hallway or I stop my car—I look and look for them. I want to tell them I'm sorry. I wish I could do more. *I tried to honor you for your family. I tried. I really did.* I dream of them. Sitting upright in their beds. They get closer and closer, infants I baptized and teens I wept with and my elders who died with their hands in mine. Their eyes are fixed. They get so close I can feel the heat of their nostrils in my hair. I wake up with my hands across my face. I lean over my wife and wait. Wait for her chest to rise. Make sure she's breathing. One time I wake her, I wake her and I ask if I'm alive. Am I here? Are you here? Do we still have time? Can we have more? Can we make it?

I think of a hundred different ways my wife could die. An arteriovenous malformation could be hidden in her brain since birth and rupture and leave her on life support. A random segment of DNA could decide to replicate with a single error and turn into a tumor. A fire, a fall, two inches of road, three inches of water, four minutes without air, a three-hundred-million-volt lightning strike—I'm seeing these rolled in by the hour, and I imagine my wife on the stretcher because God decided, God said, *"She's done. You're next."*

I tell my supervisor Jenny in our one-on-one that I'm losing my mind. Losing stable ground. Losing my faith. Losing, most of all, the idea that the world has some built-in safeguard to keep people from the worst of suffering. I'm seeing all of it. Breathing in the fumes. The universe feels haphazard and cold.

I remember the last of my faith leaving my body.

I get a call to bless a baby, one of my favorite things to do. We see so much death it is a miracle to see a birth once in a while. I walk into the room and their mother, Ophelia, is holding her three sons. They're each the size of her palm. They do not move. They do not breathe. They have been gone a long time.

"Chaplain," Ophelia says, "I need you to bless them. I need you to tell me about the life they will never have."

And she wails. She wails. Some of the noises we make in grief, they're both human and inhuman—a noise no one should ever make, but the only one we can.

Between wails, Ophelia tells me, "The surgeon had to take my uterus. I will never bear children again. These are my first and my last."

She holds up her three sons. She asks me to tell her the stories of these sons growing up, becoming good men, becoming fathers themselves, taking care of her.

I hesitate. I remember learning in our program that sometimes we need to set boundaries with our patients because their pain can be too much for us too. Maybe I listen to that. Just politely refuse. But seeing pain like this—how can I?

"Please, chaplain," Ophelia says, lifting her sons higher. "I need this. Right now, I need this."

I honor her request. I honor her sons. I tell a story that will never be lived. I weave, I spin, I make memories from oxygen. I am a story conductor. I wave my hands. I wave a wand. I do not wave this grief away, but wave it in. I am, in some sense, constructing a world for her, a universe in which her prayers are answered, where stars in the sky have formed constellations and are not distant dying light. She weeps and laughs and nods. She gasps at every turn. It's a good story, I think.

Three sons, three brothers, three fathers, from lap to graduation to grandchildren. She is weeping with a smile. Weeping her sons to life. I am pouring out every ounce of my faith for her, my understanding of a true and divinely good order, a God who is intentional and generous— and this is my only gift for her, scattered scraps made imaginary map, improvising hope. I know it is not enough. I am pulling from the bottom of my stomach, tying plot threads with the split ends of my guts. This story I sew from silk and smoke is the hope she needs. And it is the last of my faith. I use up every bit and bolt. Each word from my mouth had been a descent: she had been at the bottom of a well and I had one rope and one pulley, and as I pulled her up by my weight, I plunged into the void of her loss. I have never, ever held this against her. I was glad to give it away. For each patient, for every grieving face, I give what I have, even when it's all I have left. I bless her children. I bless her. I leave the room.

I have never left that room.

# THE CONCLUSION I DREAD

*The conclusion I dread is not "So there's no God after all," but "So this is what God's really like. Deceive yourself no longer."*

—C.S. LEWIS ON HIS WIFE'S DEATH,
FOUR YEARS AFTER MARRIAGE[1]

"The world is indifferent," I tell my group. The chaplain residents are meeting for our weekly reflection time. "That's my fear. My fear is that God doesn't hear, doesn't care. I see doctors and nurses and surgeons and even machines doing something meaningful. What does God do?"

I'm not saying anything new. I had grown up an atheist and had said this sort of thing hundreds of times. Only this time it isn't some academic playground. Not an abstract sandbox or a disagreement or a point for my side or yours. This is near depression, the theft of significance and color. But rather than through a fog, I feel as though I am seeing completely, seeing the underside of an aimless realm where atoms collide uselessly.

One of the chaplains mentions that I'm experiencing *cumulative grief*, which is exactly what it sounds like: grief accumulated secondhand, causing chemical changes in the body, building up like toxins, wearing down the soul. I'm taking it all on, getting a transference hangover.

Many of us are here, have been here, absorbing catastrophe daily, heartache in headlines televised at fingertips.

"It's more than that though," I continue. "I feel like I'm seeing things as they really are. I haven't seen a single miracle. The world has no discernible order. We are in a closed system, and we die alone."

What I feared was not that God wasn't real, but that suffering had no meaning, no significance, no witness. I could live in a godless world. I was unsure I could live in a meaningless one. A world without a god still made sense. Faith would be one less thing for me to hold. But a world without sense was unbearable. It meant nothing was holding me.

The molecules of my old beliefs, held by shoddy theological forces, were being riven by continual horror at the hospital. The more I saw, the more my faith melted like a wax thread over fire.

What would bring it back? Did I even want it back? What sort of worldview did I have that was so collapsible and combustible it didn't hold up for me or my patients?

It did come back.

But I need to tell you it was never the same. And it couldn't stay the same if I was going to keep seeing my patients, holding their stories.

After I drop "we die alone" into the lap of my group, I'm in another one-on-one with Jenny. On a sheet of paper, she draws a box and says, "This is your faith right now." She crosses out the sides and says, "It's been broken. Your box is being rebuilt. It's going to be wider maybe, or hold more, or get expanded. However it turns out, it will be different."

"I like my old box," I tell Jenny. "I could touch every wall without trying."

"I have to tell you a bad secret," she says. "Every chaplain who has ever gone through this program gets their box exploded."

At that, suddenly, we both laugh. Tears stream from my eyes. There's a name for this apparently—*trauma laughter*. Your body knows what it needs, even stretching in opposite directions, reconciling itself.

Our laughter dwindles to silence.

"So, then," I say, "I am without an anchor."

"However it goes," Jenny says, almost in a whisper, "I'm with you in it."

"I don't believe anymore," I tell my wife over dinner.

"Believe?"

"Pain, tragedy, suffering, all that stuff—none of it is *sensible*. There's no plan. There's no order. There's no G—"

I pause. I don't want to say it.

My wife holds my hand. She is about to say something. Instead she holds. I'm thankful. How many times has she seen this now? Me at the verge of peeling away, layer by layer, until I have no mast, no hull, no sails, windless and adrift in cosmic and comic endlessness. All I have is her hand.

## BREATHING ROOM IS SCREAMING ROOM

I lost my faith in two parts. The first loss was something that had to go. But the second loss was something I scrambled to keep. That first loss wasn't so bad; it was necessary even. But it was the second that was so painful it took me out.

That first loss was giving up *Pocket Theology*, the sort of world-view that offers a simplistic, theoretical framework for how everything operates. It's the sort of thing you hear from a student of textbooks, not a student of life. Pocket Theology seems to work until a scale tips. It always tips, usually when suffering enters. The absurdity of that suffering eventually outweighs any coping or comprehension. Those theological alibis get flimsy real fast. I only know this because I've seen my patients pushed to the furthest edge of sanity by trying to connect corkboard conspiracy charts, scouring their wounds for answers, or being bombarded by spiritualized one-liners. And there, any bit of pulpit speak or pep talk turns out to be as wispy as straw.

In our chaplaincy education we had classes called didactics, and in our very first one we learned about the inadequacy of Pocket Theology—or, as the didactic called it, Swiss cheese spirituality. The clichés and snappy slogans and the bless-your-heart remarks. We also learned *why* we cling to this sort of theology, not entirely from bad motives, but sincere. So sincere, it's much harder to peel away.

I still remember my first didactic because when I entered the hospital conference room with the other interns, a woman was there, screaming over a dead body on a table. The dead body was a chaplain who had volunteered to play dead. The screaming woman was a chaplain resident.

The chaplain program was a six-month internship and a yearlong residency. It felt even longer. At any given time there were about five interns and five residents. Throw a bunch of clergy of varying ages, genders, races, and faiths into a tumbler, and by the end we were supposed to emerge as gems. Or the friction would crack us. What's the saying about omelets? Can't make one without breaking a few chaplains.

A chaplain supervisor leapt into the skit. She nearly fell over the body, playing the role of a *bad chaplain*. The type of chaplain who would say insensitive, cold, crass one-liners. I would've laughed, except I had said a lot of those one-liners myself.

"Okay, look," the supervisor said, trying not to break character, "let's just do the Lord's Prayer. So your husband can go to heaven. Do you know the Lord's Prayer? Doesn't matter. Just let me do it."

"That's my son," the chaplain resident said. "Not my husband."

Some chuckled. I took notes. *Don't mix up family members. Don't force the Lord's Prayer. Don't break character.*

"Oh, your son," the supervisor said. "He looks a lot older on the table." This time the resident broke. She let out a laugh. To her credit, just one. I wrote another note. *Don't ever say "on the table."*

The supervisor continued her improv. "Our Father, not husband, hallowed be my name. Give us away, our daily bread, forgive us our trespassing, leave us to temptation, deliver this by email, for the power and the glory, amen. And—end scene."

Interns and residents and staff chaplains applauded. I was still scribbling notes. I started to applaud, but I started just as the room stopped. My hands were very loud. I looked at my hands. Everyone looked at me. Sometimes a first impression tells the whole story.

"What is wrong with this chaplain?" Phyllis asked. I wrote on a new page, *What is wrong with me?* But she was talking about the skit. Phyllis was our educator for this didactic and one of the staff chaplains. She spoke in a way that drew in every eye and ear, her every word a monumental pylon. Phyllis seemed the tallest chaplain in the room, not because we were all sitting down, but because she was complete clarity and no nonsense. She was making sure we were no longer spiritual sledgehammers, but surgeons, midwives, doulas.

We spent some time dissecting bad clichés: Why do we say them? Who are they for? What do they really mean? The chaplains called it out, plain and simple.

"An attempt to flex doctrinal fidelity by shoehorning allegiance to our half-ideas of God, or worse, a way to appease church folks and seminary types to prove we're unshaken by suffering and still uniformly subscribed to trademarked lofty dogma."

"But really it's a way to self-soothe, a sort of death denial, duct tape to keep from falling apart at mortality, more for the speaker than for the listener, to push a cushioned distance that would insulate us from emotion or frailty or collapse."

You'd think we'd have learned by now that none of these clichés work. Not for speaker or listener. They are flattening coping strategies that don't fit with the shifting dynamics of inconsolable pain.

A deadened theology doesn't serve the dead. It only gives sweet and hollow hope to the living. But I guess that's why we still use them; the sweet stuff is strong stuff.

In my residency, my supervisor and the other residents had a name for my need to wrap things up in a bow, even if the bow was only made of false hope: *Joon-Bow* (Joon being my first name). When conflict arose in our meetings, I always had to bow-tie what was happening with some final feel-good line: "But I'm so glad we're doing this work together," or "Well, I hear everyone and everyone's got a point." I had to resolve the moment like a sitcom. I defused every dispute with banter. I could never let the friction sit. I had to smother the room in false optimism. Tie up all these bows even if they were in shreds.

I quickly learned that I did this because I grew up in a turbulent home. Dishes flying, parents swinging at each other, neighbors calling the police. Every night was another stage play of violence and shouting behind slammed doors. Furniture was expendable. Blood was a regular sight. Walls were always dented. My mother once sliced open my father's forearm from wrist to elbow with her middle fingernail. My father once struck my mother so hard that her earring fell out. Tension was a taut thread in our house, nothing ever resolved, only a revolving door of glares and short fuses.

I see conflict these days and I bring out my bow-ties and Band-Aids. I don't want any more broken dishes. Just clean ones, stacked and still. I'm a peacemaker. A peace broker. A peace smuggler. If I think somebody is mad at me, if they even give me a funny twitch of an eyelash, I have to go over there and make it right. I'll bring a coffee and a backup tea if they don't drink coffee. Take both. Take my wallet and my pants. I need to correct the universe and hold it up, make it stable. Make it safe. And it's for this reason: My childhood house was always a house and never a home, and in it every childhood dream found an early grave.

A thing like that, to wrap bow-ties around everybody, is a short-term solution. It's the shortest of terms. It works as well as you would think. We suffocate in bow-ties. We drown in them. Chaplains try to come up for air. Terrible but lung-filling and life-giving air.

## SWEET HOLLOW EMPTY

But I liked the bow-ties. I needed them. I craved Pocket Theology. It kept me cozy. Tucked me in, under a blanket statement, but at least it was a blanket. Under it I believed in causality and correlation, a moral universe where it could never get *so* bad, as if the bowels of reality contained a fail-safe that could turn any pain into a bestseller, call it *The Plan All Along*.

I couldn't blame any of my patients for gripping those bow-ties either. The Pocket Theology was convenient, even essential in the first wave of crisis. Our brains reach for any framework, for promises even if they're too large to keep. It is momentary survival. It is an attempt to regain any footing. This I almost understand.

I had hoped at the center of the universe to find a benevolence into which I could dip my paintbrush and run it over every patient and every pain and every question. I was willing the world around me into the image of it that I needed. It was selfish mostly, and maybe understandable. I was trying to repair some fractured image of myself. That was faith for me. That was faith *for you*. It had to be. I was doing you a favor. Hold still. Let me wrap you up tight. Where are you going? I just want to help. Believe me. Believe this.

Faith brandished this way by those standing over the bed—whether that's me or clergy or leaders or self-help authors or the able-bodied and carefree—they often, inadvertently or not, propagate their own world-view at the expense of the wounded. Faith becomes a coat of sugar that hardens into cement. I saw this over and over at bedside, those who smeared their faith like a varnish of epoxy. I was angry about this. I was angry at myself, too, for how easily it spilled out of me. When those one-liners were thrown at the wounded, I wanted to throw my body in their path. Pocket Theology just barely worked in the hands of my patients, but when those looming at bedside came armed with it, it crushed the patients and me and the staff and, maybe even, themselves.[2]

I found that the only real way I could navigate loss was to lose this part of my faith, the part that was all sap and saccharine. And was it really a loss anyway? Or had it always been a garish garment, ill-fitting for disaster and aftermath?

Once it was gone, I could no longer wrap my patients in coats of sugar. No more bow-ties made of cement. We were left to float. A floating with no point of reference. No equations. No guarantees.

When I couldn't throw around Pocket Theology clichés anymore, I was startled: I had very little to throw around at all. There was not a single thing I could say to a suffering patient that did not burden them more. Oh, you're in pain? Here's a lifeboat called Religion. A lifeboat called Self-Help. Called Hustle-and-Grind. Called the Law of Attraction. Called Just Be Strong.

My patients tried to hold these tight. They tried. The problem was that none of these things really held them.

I thought at first that the stuff I learned in seminary would eventually get refined in the crucible of the hospital and emerge as gold. What a very romantic idea. I was sure I just needed an upgraded worldview. Get some experience in the ring, add some tools to the belt, purge all the bad clichés, and get some new moves.

It didn't go that way. My theology didn't need an upgrade. It needed disassembly. What I carried would not carry. In an air-conditioned church, maybe. In crisis, in pain? Much harder.

The defense I kept hearing was, *The theology is good, but the timing is bad. The theology is true, but you just can't say it to a hurting person right now. Save it for later when they're ready.*

When they're ready. When would that be?

If "good theology" wouldn't work in your worst moment, why should it work for any moment at all?

If it doesn't carry you in suffering, how can it carry anything else?

If it doesn't work in the end, I didn't want it now either.

Whatever you call it—pop psychology, positive thinking, chalkboard inspiration, live-laugh-love-ology—it all left my patients as empty as itself. It was all a sweet hollow empty promise.

## THREE PATIENTS, THREE QUESTIONS: THE EXPLANATION, THE EXPECTATION, THE EXTENT

That sugarcoated part of my faith had to go, and maybe I could live with that.

But this other part—the central framework for my theology of suffering—included something crucial here that I grieved giving up.

Before the last of my faith left the room with Ophelia, the mother of the triplets, I had three patients who brought me to the limits of my box.

They each asked me a question. You've probably heard them yourself. But I couldn't avoid them anymore in the maw of the hospital. It was these questions that tore the cracks in my box before the sides fell away.

My patient Jaynie asks the first question. She interrogates the *Explanation*.

Jaynie asks, "What's the reason then? I don't care if God shows up and tells me the reason, I'm still mad." She's been admitted for an MVC, motor vehicle collision. Her wife, Susie, died in the crash.

"The problem I got is this idea that *everything happens for a reason*," she continues. "I mean, yeah, it's scary to think that things *just happen*. It's so . . . sloppy. But it also means there isn't some cruel taskmaster trying to force something on me. If there's no purpose to it, I can just deal with Susie being gone. I don't have to figure out something else. *I don't have to make this hurt some big lesson.*"

Jaynie has been telling me she's stuck between two choirs. One is her church friends, telling her the usual: There's a reason for this.

God's Will. God's test. Let the pain push you to Him. She doesn't like any of it. But the other choir is her Noontime Drinking Friends, and they're not saying much different: When it storms, you dance in the rain. Don't ask for a lighter weight, get a stronger spine. At least you knew her a few years. At least you'll know what's important in life.

She's got both church culture and pop culture crowding each shoulder. Full of explanations. They're dropping Thoughts and Prayers and Good Vibes on her that she never asked for.

"The way I see it," Jaynie tells me, "maybe there's a reason for this, just like I loved Susie for so many reasons. But you know, I loved her for no reason at all. And that works for me. Does it work for you?"

My patient Raymond asks me the second question. He examines the *Expectation*.

Raymond says, "I know I'm going to heaven. But what's that got to do with me today? I know I'm saved from my sin, but this cancer hurts so bad right now."

Raymond has retinoblastoma, or eye cancer. With that come migraines, vision loss, and his remaining eye scheduled for enucleation, or surgical removal.

"Live by faith, not by sight, you know," Raymond tells me, scratching his eye patch. "But man. I want to live by sight too."

Raymond continues, "I'm forgiven. Good. Okay. Great. But what does God say about this?" He lifts up his eye patch. "What does God say about stage three cancer in my eye? I mean, you kidding?"

I think Raymond has expected his theology, the one he has been given, to work as a solid structure against crisis, but it has turned out to be shaky scaffolding only interested in reaching heaven instead of holding flesh, his illness, his agony. He is, in a sense, no better off than the man born blind in the book of John, given a moral prescription for sin but no medicine for soul. And would any moral platitudes, really, be able to touch pain so deep? What can I say to Raymond but to offer him the theology of presence and be with him as he weeps from his remaining eye?

My patient Bastian asks the third and final question.

"They told me the storm would pass. It never did. It never will. What do I do now?"

Bastian has chronic pain because of (1) an accident that required spinal fusion and (2) his sickle cell anemia. He has regular episodes of ten out of ten pain, and eventually an infection or a stroke will kill him.

He is mad about the *Extremity* of his suffering. I would be too.

"They say tragedy comes in threes," Bastian says, holding up three fingers he's unable to straighten. "That's not true. Tragedy happens whenever it wants. You think a person can't suffer more, but they can. They tell me I'm strong, but that's the problem. I just won't die." Suddenly Bastian laughs and asks me, "I know Job had it rough, but did he ever have spinal surgery?"

He recounts the dilemma of the Problem of Evil, which asks the question: *If suffering exists, how can God be good?* But really that's the wrong question, he says. Instead it should be, *I get that there's suffering, but does it really have to be this much?* It isn't that suffering exists, but the degree of suffering, its extent, that is the issue.

"It's funny, they say pain makes you stronger," Bastian tells me. "They only ask the people who survive it. Pain like the type I got? It leaves no witnesses."

His smile fades. He leans over, looks left and right, and says to me in a whisper:

"Do me a favor, please. Don't pray for me. I'm not afraid that God won't hear me. I'm afraid that God *will*."

## I WAS RIGHT ABOUT YOU ALL ALONG

What really got to me was seeing the look on my patients' faces. That look of resignation, defeat, even betrayal. I shared their exhaustion: I was done with hearing pain explained away. Done with expecting a good prognosis, a prayer answered, the numbers getting better. Angry at the extremity of their pain, the almost endless capacity for a human body to take on injury, lose blood and breath, so many compressions for nothing, have *that many* tubes and needles and tape, have so much voice to scream. I recall the words of C.S. Lewis when he lost his wife to cancer: "Reality, looked at steadily, is unbearable."[3]

I could leave behind the Pocket Theology, the Swiss cheese theology, the bad, broad-brush theology. What I couldn't stomach was what slithered underneath it—when I pulled back the slab of my faith to find an existential nightmare. A godless trembling of pulp and ooze: *We die alone. No intervention. No connection. A writhing and a sputter.*

I had been an atheist before, so I thought it was going to be easier. Losing faith should've been like taking off a scarf that was too tight. Going back should've been as easy as saying, *I was right about you all along.*

But I didn't want to be right. What I grieved, simply, was that a prayer shouted to the ends of creation would go unanswered. That I was sending letters that went unread and unreturned.

I was visiting patients of every faith and no faith, from worshipers of Vishnu to Mahavira to Buddha to Allah to Jehovah to no one. But with god or no god, there was only one common element:

The suffering was always real. It consumed cells, prayers, memories, upward mobility, youth before elder, most especially the poor, the marginalized, the disabled, the unnamed.

I found it harder to believe. Like breathing through a crooked straw. I was grasping at a scaffolding that was uneven at every end. Hope was a bad ingredient that soured the whole dish. I could do without hope. I could do zero expectations. I could deal with right now. I couldn't deal with "It'll get better."

What I grieved was my sense of safety. The universe, it seemed, was abusive. There was nothing safe about it. And while it might seem that it's punishing you, apparently it has an alibi: It is simply a matter of its material colliding with your material. Nothing more. Bad choices can land you in a hospital room, but you could have made every good choice and still end up terminal. Either way, your life vanishes into the vastness of an unthinking vacuum. Who is listening? Our prayers are radio waves but God has no antenna, no receiver, no face.

I'd see patient after patient weeping about how much it hurt. And I'd beg God at bedside, *Would you ease up a little? Can you just let up for a second? Just give my patient one damn second to breathe. Please. I'll take it. I'll take this pain. Let me take it. Can't you take it?*

It's probably easier to roll off my tongue that "I lost my faith," but it was more like, "My trust in this Person was broken." If I cobbled together the confessions of some of my patients, their confessions about how they felt about their god, I imagined they sounded like:

*You hear about somebody you're not sure about. But he tells you he's good. Your friends say the same thing. Seems true. Seems real. You trust him. You follow his advice. You expect he will follow through. It's good for a while. Real good. Lots of intimate Sundays. Lots of good being done. Lots of singing and dancing and inexplicably, fog machines. Anyway, this is the one you were looking for.*

*But sometimes he doesn't answer calls. He ghosts you on several occasions. He's always late. The blueprint doesn't look like the results. There are gaps in his story. Cracks show. You're in crisis and he's a no-show. He shows up for your friends, at least. But for you? At the hospital? Forget it.*

*You discover his actions have no real motive. Not even malice, but an uninvested flailing. He betrayed you. Not with intent, but with apathy. You want the old stories to be true. You want to believe he was always who he said he was. It was nice to believe. You finally see his face and you expect warmth and welcome. Instead you look into stone and sand. This is always who he was. Be deceived no longer. He was always unbothered.*

Most of my patients weren't even mad about this. They were hurt. Shocked, even. They had trusted, and then it was twelve failed surgeries later. Or the transplant was going to kill them. Or one of their twins died but one survived, praise God—but no, never mind, the other twin died too.

It wasn't that they expected life to go easy. They just didn't expect it to go so hard. There was not a second to breathe. Not a miracle to be seen.

## NOT A SUGAR COATING BUT A HOLY COVERING

I'm sorry to say: I have never seen a miracle.

I get asked, but no. I haven't seen one. Not in the hospital. Not in eight years there.

Most days are Friday. Friday on a cross. Friday, total chaos. Friday, only loss.

Fridays the hurt is heavy. The surgery doesn't work. Time of death is called. The disease takes it all.

The stone silence of Saturday. The confusion and shock and fear. The only sound is the sobbing. The only sight a sheet. The smell of a million plastic tubes. I want to jump to Sunday. Sunday is sealed, over and over, sealed shut.

I'm telling you the truth: I have never seen a resurrection. Only the cold of death, the irreversible.

I wish I could tell you, "And then I came back to faith when . . . ," and it was as easy as one conversation, one sermon, one Sunday.

My supervisor was right. Every chaplain I've met, me included, had their faith-box demolished. We saw too much. We grieved ideas like permanence and eternal memory and divine order. Mostly it was the idea of safety that fell away. In its place, we floated between rooms to these boxless hospital bedsides.

What I no longer believed in was any sort of worldview that had to be *held up* in order to sustain itself. No doctrine or mindset or self-improvement plan made sense to me in this place. Patients were already burdened with cancer and car accidents; I didn't need to burden them further with lectures and lessons and forced epiphanies.

The only thing I had left to believe was not a belief I had to keep, but a belief that kept me. Even if it was one moment of safety, that was what I needed. If I had to hold it up, I let it go. If it held me in that moment, that would have to do.

And the only way I've seen that we can bear the unbearable is when we bear it alongside each other. That sounds like a sappy deal, I know. But even if only for a moment, if you cover somebody with fully open hands rather than clichés or coats of sugar, you can make the grief bearable. I mean it. You really can.

A girl no older than ten is brought into the Emergency Department with deep, jagged lacerations on her back. Her shirt is shredded. Her back is really torn up, almost ribbons in several places, blood filling her shorts. She's fidgeting, squirming, but not from her injuries. She's trying to sit up, eyes darting, looking for someone. She's trying to tell something to the paramedics, to the nurses and doctors, to me.

The girl is asking, "Is my brother okay? Is he okay? He needs his medicine. His medicine."

Her five-year-old brother is brought in. They were involved in the same accident.

"He's okay," the nurse tells her. "Hardly a scratch on your brother, really." Every ten seconds, the older sister asks about her younger brother, even though she's bleeding everywhere and way worse off than her brother.

I sit down at the girl's bedside while the trauma team is swirling around her.

"You're a good sister," I tell her. "What happened?"

"I heard the inside of the car make a *boom*, like a firecracker," she says. "I knew something was wrong. I knew it! I grabbed my brother and I wrapped myself around him because I didn't want glass to get in his face."

I glance at her back, covered in cuts and bruises—and I understand.

A part of me thinks, *Thank God they're okay.* And another part of me thinks, *What a terrible world we live in, that they even have to be here.*

I feel angry that something like this had to happen to this girl and her brother, that no child is safe from destiny, from fate, from a universe where cars combust in fire and glass. But I think about the girl covering her brother, and it is right then that she unravels my knotted coldness of mindless atoms and brings me back to a glimpse of life. I hate that they have to be here. Yet my guts now stretch to this other place where this sister's unblinking reflex is powerful and real, and I see how within seeming lawless disorder, a miraculous thing can still happen. She didn't try to wrap a bow around her brother's suffering. She wrapped herself.

I see the stripes on her back. Her love for her brother. Bearing the wounds of her brother.

I have heard often that *grief is love*. But I have found, too, that love can cover grief. My faith tries to live in this place now. Between the marred landscape of our broken boxes and the possibility of the divine covering us in the starkest of our suffering. The miracle of making grief bearable by being with us in it. Still, this holds.

"You saved your brother's life." I can barely get the words out.

"But his medicine?" she asks. "You'll make sure he gets it?"

"Yes," I tell her, trying to smile through flooded eyes. "Yes. You're a good sister. What's your name?"

"Angela," she says, "but my dad calls me Angel."

Sometimes, if only slightly, I have seen the impenetrable become diffuse, just translucent enough for a stubborn sunbeam to spill through.

Sometimes we get a patient who is practically nameless. And with sheer luck and detective work, through partial ID or a random business card in a pocket, after dozens of phone calls to find next of kin, I reach a friend of a relative who knows this patient's father. I've seen reconciliation. Once in a while, Lazarus emerges from the dark.

Sometimes I hold a patient's hand as he dies. He remembers his life before he got too sick. He tells me he loved to play jazz once. The bass. He almost made it. He tells me about his band. He almost sings. I can hear his music, and he has come alive for the first time in twenty years. His final breath is a song.

Sometimes two out of three triplets will not survive. But one—one is still breathing. Somehow heart beating. She still might not make it. I've seen so many die. But this baby is a resurrection. A stoneless tomb. For now, she is almost a miracle. Almost.

Once in a while, I have seen the stone roll back, even an inch, and I see the barest hint of light. It can look like one phone call, a gentle face, a new pulse.

I'm not sure I've seen a miracle, at least not somebody gasping back to life on a table. But I might have seen enough light to pierce a room, a deathbed, a tomb.

*Part Two*

# LOSING MIND

*three*

# LOSS OF MENTAL HEALTH: ALL WE COULD HAVE DONE

## On the collective cost of losing our mental health

Content warning: This chapter contains descriptions of depression and suicide. Reader, please be advised.

*My friend, just think about it one more time.*

—INSCRIPTION ON A BRONZE STATUE OF ONE MAN
COMFORTING ANOTHER, OVER HAN RIVER IN SOUTH
KOREA. HAN RIVER HAS OVER FIVE HUNDRED
SUICIDE ATTEMPTS REPORTED PER YEAR.[1]

"I'm mad at him, but I miss him," Marcus tells me.

I'm called to my patient Marcus because he needs to talk about his friend Lamar, who has just taken his own life.

Lamar had spiraled into depression again, and it had finally won. He had set up a novelty sword in his living room, held fast by an assortment of chairs, tables, desks, and duct tape, and then fell on the sword.

"You ever heard anything like that?" Marcus asks, voice rasping. "It's a brutal way to go."

Then he says a familiar thing I've heard. An echo.

"What if I had just—"

*—reached out to him one more time, picked up the phone, stopped by, checked in, paid attention, grabbed some lunch, been more encouraging, set a date, made some time—*

"—but would that have worked anyway?"

As simply as I can say it: *When a mind suffers inside, every heart around it suffers with them too.*

Mental health is inextricably linked with our communal health. A few doors down, a few cars over, across the dinner table, you know someone who is sinking.[2]

If you are the one sinking, the one whose brain is wounded, it is always hardest on you. You experience incalculable loss in not being able to trust your own mind. And if you are the beloved community witnessing your loved one slip into an internal, invisible trap door— this is nearly as hard. Not the same, but still, pain.

Each time I've fallen back into depression, it seems that those I love are pulled into its gravity. I assume that when others reach in to help, I am inviting them into quicksand. I lose parts of myself and so it forces others to fill in those gaps. I want them to step in, and I don't. I become a matter of concern, soon a liability, then a burden.

Becoming a burden this way opens up a two-way street of guilt. My guilt is that each moment my community spends with me is another moment they lose for themselves. Their guilt is that they want to do more but they have to do less: The land of the living cannot stop for either of us.

My grief is over all the ways I am drained and am draining others.

Their grief is that they are helpless in seeing me helpless.

I will always advocate for this: *to stay*. Stay for the afflicted. Stay and be. No one ought to run at the first sign of trouble. It is human to intervene and to reach hands in for the wounded.

I believe deeply, always, in staying. It is my life's work. More than that, it is the work of life.

But what I hadn't been told is that there is a romanticized, over-wrought version of staying. The version in which we believe that giving over everything will rescue or cure or save. It's an understandable hope. A hope turned in on itself. A hope built on a falsely glorified altar of *sacrifice*, the idea that enough of our blood will trip a cosmic wire that can stop a soul from turning ghost. That it all depends on us.

The opposite idea is that stepping back, even for a little while, equals monstrous abandonment. We get taught this early. To give, and give, give more, because you never know, *or else*. We give away the bricks of our foundation because we're told it's the noble thing. All the while our own frame collapses into every space we used to be.

If you know this tension, neither choice is fair, right, good. And you grieve either way.

What I've seen is that there is no such thing as deciding between *stay* or *go*. A person who loves the afflicted, in some sense, is *always* staying. They stay in worry, in guilt, in fear, in *what-if*. And a person who loves the afflicted is *always* going. They go each time they have to go back to work, back home, back to life, back to their own.

To stay or go: We pay a cost.

I wish I could give you some hope about this. From my time at bedside, I've found just one thing. There's a part of this grief around mental health that I need to tell you about. I'm afraid it could make it worse, like I'm only describing the fog and not a way out of it. But maybe if I tell you what I've seen, I can point you to a little less guilt, a little more grace, some way of real forward movement.

## ALL IT TAKES IS EVERYTHING

*Depression is hard on friends. You make what by the standards of the world are unreasonable demands on them, and often they don't have the resilience or the flexibility or the knowledge or the inclination to cope. If you're lucky some people will surprise you with their adaptability. You communicate what you can and hope. Slowly, I've learned to take people for who they are. Some friends can process a severe depression right up front, and some can't. Most people don't like one another's unhappiness very much.*

—ANDREW SOLOMON, *THE NOONDAY DEMON*[3]

The summer of 2020, my daughter is born. A month before in June, I had marched for Black lives, chanting the names of George Floyd and Breonna Taylor. Four months before that in March, the week of my birthday, ten US states had confirmed cases of a mysterious virus. My daughter arrives in a world of heightened violence and anxiety.

My wife tells me three weeks after our daughter is born that she wants to exit.

"Exit?"

"I want to leave. Living. I want to exit."

She schedules with her physician to discuss postpartum depression. The clinic is slow. Summer days are long. We have no visitors. No extra hands. I am on a six-week medical leave to be at home. *We'll make it*, I think. *I know we'll make it.* I am making meals, cleaning up, feeding and changing our daughter, changing my wife. My wife sticks close to the walls. We get curtains that shut out the sun.

My wife's physician refers her to a psychiatrist. The week before the appointment, on a feverish and frantic night, I wake up to noise in the kitchen. In the dark, I see my wife opening a bottle of pills. I run to grab the bottle from her hands. She fights me. "Let me exit," she says. "I have to exit." There is nothing in her eyes. I don't want to grab her hands, her arms. I have no other way of taking this bottle from her. Her fingers are steel. It's only my desperation that manages to pry her hands open. Do you know this feeling? The impossibility of pushing someone out of traffic without hurting them? I beg her to live. Our daughter startles awake and cries.

My wife sees her. Sees me. For a while, I grip the bottle of pills between us.

I tend to our daughter, holding the bottle of painkillers in my armpit, hands shaking in purple moonlight. My only thought is that I will take care of us. I will give my life doing it. But the question hangs: *Can I?*

I'm at the bedside of a woman who has set herself on fire, not for the first time. Her husband and daughter are there. The woman, Brinda, is intubated. Inhalation injury, second-degree burns, skin graft scheduled the next day. Her husband says to me, through tears and clenched fists, "Let me be really honest here, chap. I'm sick of this. I'm sick of her. The first dozen times, I had adrenaline, I had my love for her. I tried everything. But I, *we*"—he points to his daughter—"We can't. We can't anymore."

He tells me every time she has set herself on fire, their entire world went up in flames. Their compassion eventually cooled to contempt. They burned through all their savings for therapy and medication and vacations and seminars and retreat centers and life coaches and a home health aide. They're trying. But they're so tired.

"It's an ugly feeling, chap. I know. Makes me want to throw up. The guilt. The nurse said you wouldn't judge me. You don't, right? Because I do."

## PLEASE LOOK AFTER ME, AFTER YOU

I throw away every bottle of painkillers in the house. I hide a few of the pills. For me. At the virtual psychiatrist appointment, the doctor diagnoses my wife with PPD, postpartum depression, and immediately invokes the Baker Act. It's a mandatory seventy-two-hour hold for someone who expresses thoughts of self-harm.[4] I only know about it because I went through it over twenty years ago after I swallowed half a bottle of pills. I was taken from the hospital to a facility with caged windows and dozens of other patients, all of us prisoners. Ten years ago I had a friend who was "Baker Acted" by two police officers in front of me, led away in handcuffs, sent to a hospital for a day, and then put back on the street.

In response to the Baker Act, a police officer is sent to our home. To take my wife by force to a random hospital for a three-day hold. My wife begs me to send him away. She is insistent that she will not be escorted by police in full view of our neighbors while I remain with our newborn. I am not sure what to do. I cannot make her go. But how do I have her stay? I only know she will not go this way. With a mask and shield on my face, I spend half an hour persuading the officer that my wife doesn't need to be taken. He stands in our living room, no mask, a hand on his holster. Everything skips a frame. I can hear the blood moving in my mouth. The officer is convinced. He gets in his car and watches our house for a while before leaving. Then my wife asks me about going to a private facility instead. A nice retreat center, stay a few weeks, regain ground. We almost make the payment. The whole time, our daughter cries. My wife changes her mind. I want her to go. But she has just enough mind to tell me she will not. Should I make her? Or must I honor her autonomy, even if it is just a shred? What can I do? I stay. I take another six weeks off work. I will be home for twelve weeks.

Our daughter cannot stop crying. She might have colic. She has tremors. She might have cerebral palsy. I do not sleep. I run between my wife and daughter. My arms are never at rest, only extended. My wife turns to me every hour and asks if she can exit. She says nothing else.

After my wife's diagnosis, I am strong for seven full weeks. I've slept, at most, three hours a night. But I can keep doing this. I will take care of us. I will give my life for it. Love can keep me going. It has to. Can it?

My wife enters a different stage of her depression. Each morning, out of sheer anxiety, she scratches my torso with her nails. At first, I let her. But I only have so much blood. We try to come up with a list of "activities" each day. They're really distractions. Her anxiety gets her to finish the list before noon. Soon she picks fights. Yells, slams doors, demands more Advil. She finds the ones I hid, and I have to grab them again. She tells me I'm a bad husband. A bad human being. A bad person, she keeps saying, "You're a bad person." She tells me that marrying me was a mistake.

Then on week seven, I hear music. Loud music. I hear my daughter crying. I hear her in the next room. I run between hallways looking for her. I look for a piano. Who is crying? Our daughter? My wife?

When did we get a piano? I see a figure running. He turns. I am chasing myself. That's when I know: I'm hallucinating.

I pack a few things. I don't want to leave. I can't. I just need a break. Just some time. I flee home for a night. I strike myself in the face. A coward, I'm a coward. I want to stay but I'm afraid of myself. Afraid of this home where a shadow in the kitchen is looking for pills. Afraid of seeing my ghost chasing my ghost. Afraid of this place where I can hear my child crying from every corner. The thought is here now: *I want to exit too.* I drive for hours. I sleep in my car.

I will never leave. What sort of monster would I be if I left? No one would understand. Me neither.

But to stay: What will I become if I stay? No one that anyone could recognize. Me neither.

I pray angry. Why. Why did you make a brain like this. A brain that can sabotage itself with such precision. Why did you plant a time bomb in our frontal lobes. What did I do to get such a curse. Why after a mother giving birth. Help us. Help me. Please help.

I search online for help.

There's a study that shows eleven men who "survived" their wives' PPD. I should be more understanding but maybe I'm tired; the more I read, the angrier I get. These men divorce or leave or complain the whole time. I can only judge them. Then I get the idea that I'm only angry at myself. These stories feel too close, too exposing. Their guilt is mine.

I find a blog post written by a man who lost his wife to PPD. The first line I read: "Then I found her body." I look away. I read parts of a book where a man stays with his wife for five years through her bipolar disorder. His wife is continually hospitalized. They have children. They make it. It's very romantic. That night I wrestle another bottle of pills from my wife. She has been hiding them. Can I do this for five more years? Nights, minutes, seconds? I'm determined. I won't leave. I won't. I almost believe it.

One of the things my wife keeps seeing online is "Baby Bounce Back" type stuff. New mothers are running marathons a week after giving birth. Going back to "pre-baby weight" instantly. My wife infinite scrolls, looking at photo shoots of new parents taken before the world locked down. She hates these people. She wants to be these people. She drowns in the grief of missing out on what she "should be"—she's convinced this is what it means to make it.[5]

It's October. It's back: the knife pain in my ribcage. Anxiety. Panic attacks. I ask my doctor for help. I beg to go into her clinic for an in-person appointment; I enter fully geared up, double-mask, gown, gloves. My doctor tells me her husband is dying of cancer. The appointment turns into me being a chaplain for her. I can't help myself. I run to grief. I run to stop people from exiting. As I'm leaving the office, I change masks and my doctor sees my face. Across the hall, she takes down her mask for a moment. She says to me, "Hey. I see it. The anxiety in your face. Call my cell anytime." I break down weeping in the hallway. Besides the officer I had to persuade out of my home, I had not seen another human face since my daughter was born.

In November, we celebrate 백일 (baek-il: one hundred days), the traditional Korean milestone of marking a child's first hundred days. It is said this celebration arose from a time of great scarcity in Korea when the infant mortality rate was very high. It was a rarity and good fortune that any child would survive past one hundred days. In our 백일 photos, I am smiling. Inside, hardly surviving. We look so good on social media. Alive, almost.

I have this nightmare. A regret. When our daughter was born, I had rushed the nurse to send us home early. I was afraid we'd contract the virus. Really, I think I just wanted to be home, in my own comfort. A selfish thing. It was too early for my wife. She needed the time. We left a day earlier than our expected stay. It must have been this extra day. In my nightmare, I watch me and my family leave the hospital and walk into a fog. I yell to come back. I'm sorry. Please come back. I chase them. I hear our daughter. I see my wife's hand, and every time I reach for it, she pulls away. Please, one more day. One more day of my life for yours.

I'm on medication. Buspirone fills me with rage; my palms bleed from my fingernails. I change to fluoxetine. I'm so tired, it's hard to tell if it's helping. My wife begins medication. We sit down with our daughter and my wife tells her, "I'm sorry, honey. I'm sorry I can't breastfeed you anymore. I have to take this medicine. I have to get better. Mommy will try to live." We save one pouch of breast milk in the freezer. Maybe for when our daughter is sick. Or maybe this is my wife's way of keeping part of herself alive.

It's December. My wife is recovering. My wife will be okay. I celebrate. I try to celebrate. A part of me is poisoned by guilt, ashamed by my selfishness, by having had those thoughts of running away. Another part of me is ill from the dread and terror that have filled my stomach, watching my wife be replaced by a shadow. Then back to the guilt, a circular self-bludgeoning. I spiral between these two notes: the guilt, the trauma.

The week of Christmas, I spiral. I relapse from a fifteen-year sobriety. I drink a bottle of wine. We had saved it for a Christmas gift. The bottle plus the antidepressants plunge me into a psychotic episode. My wife stays up with me as I rattle off a stream-of-consciousness monologue about every single trauma I faced in my childhood. I talk like this for hours. The morning hits our sunproof windows.

From the shadow of the curtains, I see myself. "You made it," he tells me. I see my shadow in my periphery, in the kitchen, the hall, my daughter's room. "You made it," he keeps saying. Pressed against my ear, my eyes open deep into the night, he says again and again: "You made it. You. You. But me. This part of you. Did not."

My wife hardly remembers this time. A fragment might return. In some way, maybe her memory loss is a hidden mercy. Maybe her brain protected her from the trauma of those months. I don't begrudge her that. I don't begrudge her any of it. I'd rather she forgets. There is no comparison: She had it hardest. I was a cameo in her survival.

But we both grieve this time. She grieves the forgetting. I grieve the remembering. She grieves that she could not be the mother she wanted to be. She grieves those months she cannot remember our child, those fresh smells, her first laughter, the shape of her first words. There is also an incursive paradox: She regrets she could not be there for me during her depression.

My regret is that I wish I could have done the impossible: to give more.

I visit Marcus again, my patient who has lost his friend Lamar.

"Chap, this isn't good," Marcus tells me. "This will sound nuts but I . . . I think I caught Lamar's issues. Is it contagious? Like a flu?"

I want to tell him that this is not uncommon: Grief can give way to PTSD, major depression, anxiety, or "funeral mania." Those already afflicted with mental illness suffer even more severely when their loved ones die.[6] But I've also questioned: Does this further stigmatize grief? Pathologize grief as a mental illness? If I scream at a funeral, am I suddenly diagnosed with funeral mania?[7]

The best I can reply to Marcus is,

"I'm no therapist, but I think—if you miss your friend—you're grieving. Grieving can be depressing."

"So you're saying it's contagious, but with more words?"

I chuckle, nervously. "I guess it's contagious like . . . like doing good is contagious. Or laughing. Or yawning. Or optimism, maybe."

"So you sneeze depression and I catch depression? That sounds bad. Just terrible."

"Uh. Well. I guess I'm trying to say that it's normal to feel this way."

"Dang, chap. I don't know though. I don't feel *normal*."

"What I mean to say is, it's not *wrong* you feel this way."

"Yeah? But I *feel* wrong."

I'm sweating. These visits sometimes feel like we are two voices stumbling to harmonize, wires crossed, figuring out our vocabulary and history and symbols. Fits and starts, words slipping off cliffs, it can take a while, and it doesn't always get there, and I had been wondering if this would be a visit where I'd fail to connect. It happens. These visits are microcosms of all our attempts to find each other, the way that a single phrase can bridge us, or how one word can send us back to the precipice. And two people just talking: That whole thing is never easy if you've ever tried it. Half my job is working through the sweating.

Marcus, thankfully, is determined. I'm thankful for patients who give me wide room to falter.

"Chap, don't worry," he says with a wink. "I got a therapist. In case it gets bad."

I exhale. A long one. Marcus, with grace I can't believe, tries again.

"Chap? One more question. You don't have to answer but . . . you ever lost anyone like Lamar?"

"Yes," I reply. "At least five people."

"Did you ever get over it?"

"Honestly, I—no. No, I didn't. I wish I could tell you that I did. But I'm not sure I want to get over it."

Marcus closes his eyes. "That's okay with me. It's like I *want* to feel messed up about this. I mean, you said it, love is contagious, right?"

I hadn't said it. I slowly nod yes. He shakes his head no. I shake my head no. We both laugh.

Marcus continues. "Real serious though, chap. I'm not getting over anybody. Somebody's sad, I'm sad. He's happy, I'm happy. I'm sad he's gone. So, I'm sad he's gone. I'll keep it that simple." I see a tear, just one, from duct to cheek to chin. "Yeah. Yeah, man, I miss him. I was so mad at him. I was more mad at myself. I was mad I didn't get to him in time. Then—you know what, chap? I don't know if I'm right about this, but I had to forgive myself. Not all the way. But I want to think he wouldn't hold it against me. Probably that's wishful thinking. Really wishful."

I want to jump in and tell Marcus, *"He wouldn't hold it against you."* But I pause. See the one tear. See Marcus's eyes closed, eyes working, moving through the hard and unsolvable pain of losing a friend this way. Every punishing thought. Bit of anguish. Ounce of guilt. He senses he's not worthy to grieve his friend, because his friend is the one who was taken and yet he himself is still alive. This is complicated grief. More than complicated. It's a loop that will never close, a tear that may never drop. Grief suspended. I hold here. Here is all I can hold.

He opens his eyes. "You can say a prayer, if you want to."

"What's the biggest thing I can pray about for you right now?"

Marcus full-on weeps. He says, "Is it true we can't pray for the dead? Can you still pray for Lamar? Just that he's at rest, finally? That he's been put right? Please. Please pray for my friend. My best friend Lamar. He's the best person I ever knew and I hope he forgives me. Lamar, man. *Man.*" Marcus puts a hand on his chest, closes his eyes again. "Why did you do this, man? I'd take it from you. I'd take your place in a second. You were my boy, Lamar. Be easy, man. I miss you out here."

# ALL WE COULD HAVE DONE IS DONE

Here's what I want to tell you, to offer some hope, as bleak as it may be.

*You tried to get care, you tried to offer care,*
*but each time you needed more help,*
*you found less help, and even less of yourself.*

In other words: *Every failure to get help was not on you. You were depleted before you got there.*

Is that too simple? Here's what I mean:

I visit a patient I've seen before. Brinda, the woman who set herself on fire. She is intubated again. She is about to go CMO, Comfort Measures Only. She will soon be terminally extubated.

Her family and friends surround her. I stand at bedside to offer Commendation of the Dying, or what was once called last rites. The family doesn't mind that I'm not Catholic. They want anything. Prayer, ritual, oil, words, water. Anything. Everything.

If you were to spin a camera from the middle of the room, the first person you'd see is Brinda's husband, Terrell. He is holding a fist against his chest, his open hand on Brinda's head. Clenching his teeth, his fist. I've seen this look, when someone needs to weep but won't. At my last visit, Terrell told me he couldn't take any more days off work or he would lose their insurance. His work had barely covered the bills. But his guilt is that he had to work so much to keep his wife alive, he couldn't be there for her as much as he wanted to. A stomach-sick choice. He doesn't know if he did it right. But he hates that he had to choose.

Pan the camera slightly left. Brinda's daughter, Ilana, is in a chair. Her jaw is hardened. She's holding her mother's hand. Ilana has told me she's run out of tears to cry. *Just numb now, I ran out.* Ran out of tears, ran out on her mom. She is in college going on her sixth year. She had to redo a few semesters because she had run out of classrooms at each of her mother's hospitalizations. During the last one, she ran from her mom instead. Ilana has finally chosen herself first—but now here her mother is, breathing her last.

Move the camera again. Brinda's brother, Yosef, is at bedside, both hands gripping the back of his own neck. He tells me he knew early on that his sister was "in a bad type of way. When she was a kid she was always off to the side, in her own head." But Yosef says he doesn't believe in all this "depression stuff."

"Talking about it makes you depressed," he insists. He kept telling his sister to try yoga or painting or herbal tea and "This will pass." Yosef has flown across the country to be at bedside. This is the first and last time he's visiting his sister at the hospital. Yosef's wife took the week off to watch their two young children at home. But Yosef has had to stay an extra week. "Probably gonna lose my job," Yosef tells me, "and now my wife might lose hers."

The other side of the bed: Brinda's best friend, Jalene, is sobbing loudly, shaking. Jalene tells me she was there for Brinda when her daughter, Ilana, was born. Brinda had PPD, so Jalene became an impromptu auntie. "I'd do it again," she says. Most of Brinda's friends left. "They should've stayed, but that's not my business. Everybody's got a mortgage,

I guess." Jalene also tells me, "I know they had to go. You try to help somebody when they're hurting, but if they bite your hand every time, you have to go. Especially if you need those hands for your own thing."

Behind Jalene is Janice. Janice is the home health aide, hired for wound care to treat all of Brinda's burns. Janice has known Brinda and her family for years. Some of the family tells me that Janice is an honorary auntie, like Jalene: available outside hours, in constant communication with the primary physician and psych and case workers, always looking up more resources. Janice shares the frustration that every healthcare worker has: "I went out of my way, made so many calls to find the right help, but it just goes in a big circle. The system is stretched so thin, there is no system. You have to be almost dead to get help. You're lucky even then if you get it."

Suddenly I get a flashback. I remember my *halmuni*, my grandmother, who eventually lost her brain to dementia, who shouted at ghosts in the kitchen while smoke filled our home because of the squid she had left roasting in the oven. I remember my uncle, who had paranoid delusions, and he would randomly get on a bicycle and pedal from Florida to California; he believed he was being hunted all the time, and he stuck dry beans in his ears to stop the voices. I remember our family trying to apply for disability, for any government assistance, but my grandmother and uncle didn't meet the criteria because *they weren't disabled enough.* My mother couldn't afford her mother's care anymore, so our *halmuni* was put in a SNF, a skilled nursing facility. In a few months she died, not knowing her own name. It is my mother's deepest regret.

A last camera move. The person next to me is Brinda's father, Bruce. He's a widower. His wife, Shania, Brinda's mother, took her own life a decade ago. Bruce tells me, "I'll never understand it. They went through it. But it means I gone through it too. I tried to keep the lights on. And for what? House with lights on and nobody home—that's not a home."

What I'm seeing in my dying patient is more than her death, but the death around her. The death of her family's capacity to be present. Stolen by every demand, every deadline, a thousand small deaths that ripped them away. They grieve their beloved; they grieve that they could not choose to be with her as much as they wanted to.

Did the community fail? Or really, has it been set up for failure?

Can you really be blamed for the ways you could not support, reach in, reach out?

I cannot blame you, not myself, in a choiceless world. At the deathbeds of the afflicted, I only feel a quiet and intense anger at how we must endure this capitalist machinery, its merciless engine. Even when we want to show up, our hands are demanded elsewhere, so much that we cannot reach out to those closest to us.

Still, and still—through the gears and spokes of these imperative forces, I am a witness to those of us who break through. As best we can, to be hands and heart in a hardened world. And I know I am one of the lucky ones. I have a community who has stayed. I was alone through a lot of it. But not all of it. I was held.

I see text messages from friends when my wife had PPD. Messages that asked what we needed. I remember food at the door. I remember how much my bosses listened, heard my tears, moved heaven and earth to give me extended leave.

I remember when our friends came over with masks on and installed those sunproof curtains. We needed sleep. Those curtains, no kidding, probably saved our lives. Another friend came by to clean our home, mopped floors and cleared countertops and organized drawers. I remember when my brother-in-law and his wife sent us prepackaged meals, days and nights of food, and even though our taste was so diminished that those meals tasted like salted cardboard, we were thankful for an empty sink and full stomachs. I remember my brother, a lifetime ago, visiting me when I was under a Baker Act, cracking a joke that got us laughing through the night. His presence has held.

I remember when a church elder came by with full protective gear on to see our daughter from several feet away, and even though this elder didn't know what we were going through at home she suddenly told my wife, "It's good to use formula. All my children grew up on formula; that whole breastfeeding thing is overrated." It was a right word at the right time. Of all the unsolicited advice we got as new parents, this was the only piece that spoke to my wife's grief.

I remember texting my friend and fellow chaplain Sam the first time I was depressed during my wife's PPD. He called me immediately. I was outside on an empty sidewalk, the moon peeking out from the clouds, breathing vapor. I told him the shame I felt, the anger, the absurdity that I was making this about me. Sam asked, "What would happen if you weren't the strong one?" I remember the terror of that question. I remember weeping in relief. He had named it. It was enough for a night to hear someone name the thing I couldn't.

I've been lucky. I'm lucky to weep those kinds of tears.

And it wasn't until months after I started antidepressants that I noticed something.

I hadn't thought about taking my own life for a while. For weeks.

I used to think about it every single day. I had thought that was normal. But the medication was working.

I don't know if the next episode of depression will win. Depression

70

can be terminal, as they say. Will the very fact of living be enough to stay alive? Is it possible to hold my breath by breathing?

They say that *connecting with others* is also self-care, to improve mental health. I believe this is true, but I will add this: *Connecting is not the buffer. Connecting is the point.* I long for this to be the norm: community not as a means to survive my own life, but to be life itself. In that, I have been lucky. Through the iron grid of our world machine, which too frequently keeps us from each other, I have seen my community elbow their way in. I have seen how good can enter, as simple as hands holding me up when the floor slides away, as simple as a solid shoulder when I sway. I know that a fully present community is not a cure, and I know that medication saved my wife and my life. But our community, our village, our connection, to reach out and be reached out to, as much as we can in a fast and crushing terrain, is not just a way to keep living, but is its very own flourishing.[8]

## THE PART OF YOU THAT WANTS TO LIVE

*gezinsverpleging: a Dutch word that translates to "family nursing," a model of de-institutionalized care for mental health seen in Geel, Belgium. It was reportedly inspired by St. Dymphna, the patron saint of those with mental illness. For hundreds of years, families have hosted individuals with psychiatric conditions to care for them*[9]

My patient, who goes by Nitro, has told the nurse he has a specific plan to take his own life. He asks for a chaplain. I arrive and the entire nursing station gives me a look. *You got this,* is the look. *We trust you, chaplain.* I'm anxious. But I nod. It's all I can do not to sweat down my tie.

For those afflicted, my responsibility is this simple and this hard: *I am responsible for this moment.*

Nitro, like so many others with mental illness, tells me about his history of abuse. He eventually aged out of foster care. He now lives on disability and he has episodes of pain so bad that he begs God to be done.

Nitro lets out a breath. That long breath. It's always the one after a patient says everything, sometimes for the first time. You may have let out that breath before, the one your lungs needed to release. You might have been surprised by how much your lungs had to hold.

"My broken brain," Nitro says, "is really a busted heart." He rolls his eyes hard. "I'm sorry about this. My God. Tell me the truth, am I the worst patient you've had today?"

I tell him he's my first patient of the day. "Which means so far, no."

Nitro turns his head to the side, then laughs. He laughs until he cries. He cries until he laughs again.

After a pause, I ask him a question. "Can I make a contract with you? Can you promise to tell someone if you're going to make a decision you can't take back?" It's a risk. Contracts like this are no guarantee. If anything, it's a single expression of care, throwing a line in the water.

"Do I have to sign something?" He laughs again. Then his body changes. A very slight shift in his shoulders, almost imperceptible. "I can promise that. How about I promise that I call you?"

I think on this. I'm remembering all the stuff about provider-to-patient roles, boundaries, professionalism. Providers are not patients' friends. Nitro gives me a look. I know the look:

*I trust you, chaplain.*

"Yes," I tell him. "You can call the chaplain office. Ask for me."

Over the next few months, Nitro calls me at the office. About every two weeks he is heaving in tears, sometimes a panic attack, sometimes telling me he's done with it all. I beg him to live. Like I've begged my wife. Like I've begged my friends who are gone. Like I've begged myself. By the end of each call, we're both drained. I'm not sure if I've helped, or if I'm enabling, or if this is right. When he calls the next time, I assume that I did help the last time—but if he's calling me this time, did I really help the last time?

Nearly a year after we first met, I realize I haven't heard from Nitro in months. On an evening, a blue sunset, I wonder if I should call him. As if he knows what I am thinking, Nitro calls me. And no kidding, I can hear him smiling. No heavy breathing. No fear, no terror. He has something to say to me.

"Had to say thanks, chaplain. You. You know what you did? You saved my life. You did."

I try to tell him I didn't.

"No, sir, no," he says. "Look. I know that's a lot on you. But listen, chap. If I make it just another day, just one more day that I can stand living—it's because of you. I might not make it past the week. But another day, you helped me live. Isn't that okay? Isn't that fine? Just one more day? Do you like that or what?"

My eyes fill. I consider the weight of all he is saying. I think on our phone calls, how I was shaking scared, but how he always ended each call by saying, "Thank you for picking up when you did."

I consider how I have shared the same sort of gratitude with my village around me. I consider how I have lived on borrowed time. I consider how it was loaned to me generously by so many. Maybe they were shaking, too, hoping they had given enough. I don't resent those who couldn't give anymore. They hardly had time of their own. And I consider how many friends have lost themselves to their own minds. How much I miss them. How I know, for certain, it was never their fault. I wonder, *How am I here when they're gone? Is this fair?* I don't think it is. I can only be thankful. I have been fortified by those willing to extend their roots to strengthen mine. I consider the words of Saint Paul, "If one part suffers, every part suffers with it; if one part is honored, every part rejoices with it."[10] When my mind was afflicted, my body was my people, moving in to hurt with, to live with. Each day I am alive, I can tell you it's not because I made it—we did. I am here because you are here.

"Yes," I tell him. "I like that. I like that just fine."

"Thank you," he says, "for one more day."

*four*

# LOSS OF WORTH:
# WHAT YOU DESERVE

On abuse, trauma, survival, and
unearthing buried worth

Content warning: This chapter contains descriptions
of abuse, child abuse, physical violence, and
images of war. Reader, please be advised.

*Only through mourning everything that she has lost
can the patient discover her indestructible inner life.*

—JUDITH L. HERMAN, *TRAUMA AND RECOVERY*[1]

## (NO) SYMPATHY FOR THE DEVIL

I'm not exactly sure when it happened, but after enough night shifts,
I started to believe in monsters.

Sometimes I'd look them in the eye, but most of the time I'd see
the handprints they left behind. It was always a night shift. A victim

would be admitted under stars and moon, ambulance lights through a window. I'd get the consult for crisis assistance. If the victim was still awake and alert, they'd tell me their story. Slowly at first: *Can I trust you?* Then the thread was pulled fast. Ink spilled as quick as it could go. By the end, I knew I had been a witness to horror.

Soon a pattern emerged. It was one I knew too well. But at the hospital I saw its real scale, its intractability. A victim would tell me about their history of abuse, but then they'd describe a larger monstrosity. Victims who escaped a haunted house went on to see that the night was haunted too. If you've been there like I've been there, you know this grief: the fatigue and futility of trying to tell your story but only getting apathy instead. It's monsters all the way down.

I wish I could tell you this isn't true, but I've met monsters—and I've seen all the ways they are fed and hidden.

A young child is dropped off at the Emergency Department. The family drives off. The physicians and nurses try everything. Nothing works. They can only offer comfort in their patient's—this child's—final moments.[2]

We have a patient in the trauma bay who's been assaulted by her boyfriend on their anniversary. Her boyfriend has apparently snuck in to continue assaulting her. The patient asks me later if I can call her boyfriend. "Can you tell him I'm not mad at him?"

I catch flashes of nightmarish stories: grandparents abusing both children and grandchildren; thrown pots of boiling water; assault via gardening tool, or brick, or machete; a drunk driver suing the family of the victim he's killed for damages to his own car; horrific cases of sexual assault enabled by family members.

I want to tell you that all of this is nuanced and multilayered, and I want to tell you that abusers are often also abused themselves and that generational trauma and poverty and the carceral system and a lack of education all converge into a perfect storm that results in these horror stories. All of this is true.

But it doesn't make this any less true:

*I have met monsters.*

Night after night of this, I have grieved how deep this evil runs. The more abuse I saw—the sheer magnitude of how much a victim suffered—the more I gave up trust. Trusting in anyone good. Smiles only hid knives. Success was camouflage. Imagine calling an emergency contact only to learn that they're the reason for the emergency.

What I had been trying to offer a victim of abuse, I discovered, was not only very little, but ultimately very wrong. It wasn't just the platitudes that were wrong. But I kept running up against the limitation of *forgiveness* and *nuance* and *reconciliation*. Or at least their false versions. They were replaced by something else—not a solution, but the whole picture.

## YOU CAN'T LEAVE A HAUNTED HOUSE WHEN THE HOUSE IS EVERYONE

My patient Kendie tells me her story. Her husband systematically severed every relationship she had: friends, church, coworkers, parents, siblings, and eventually her children. She apologizes for speaking slowly; her speech impediment is one of a dozen marks he left on her. She's outrun him now for a year. But, she says, he always finds her.

"The worst part wasn't even losing everyone," Kendie says. "The worst part was that he told me I was a daughter of Baal. He said I couldn't be saved. That God won't even look in my direction. I believed him. I still believe him."

She tells me it wasn't just the bruising, but the *branding*. It wasn't just about what happened, but what it says about her. Her husband has left her with a story about herself. A false one, but it has stuck. A story-stake through the heart. In that sense, she believes a religious lie about herself. About her body, her soul.

Physical abuse is usually visible in the Emergency Department. But spiritual abuse is harder to spot, insidiously hidden. It's the lie that you deserve your abuse. If someone can persuade you that *God has willed it*, then this becomes a route by which every other abuse can be smuggled into your life: verbal, physical, sexual, financial. And the lie is falsely reinforced by the very fact that the abuse happened.

Put another way, spiritual trauma is as if your body is a house and that house is haunted—and you are convinced that God is the ghost. And what begins in the body reaches inside, digs with barbed cables, hooking the soul with this toxic telegram: *My abuse says something is fundamentally wrong with me. Somehow I deserve these bruises because I have these bruises. Some sick part of me must be attracted to this evil.*

Even without religious language, abuse gets spiritual in nature. You become convinced you are cursed: *This happened to you because you deserve it, and you deserve it because it happened to you.*

This circular logic runs through every dysfunctional power structure. Kendie tells me that the one time she called the police, the officer only spoke with her husband. She tried to tell the officer, "I was also spiritually abused." The officer shook his head, left the door open as he left.

"He didn't believe my bruises," she says. "But when I told him I was spiritually abused, that's when he thought I was crazy. Religious abuse—that's not against the law, you know that? You can't report it. No one gets stopped for it. Nobody believes it's a thing."

If anything, Kendie says, her church kept hushing her because *it would look bad for everybody.*

Between us, I recognize the smoke that chokes the air. It's pervasive. In every lung and down every alley. The smoke of *enabling.* The obstinate framework of policy and authorities that will not redress her bruises, will not offer recourse, but only a phone call to her emergency contact—the abuser.

The grief of every victim is that they are mired in a perpetual current that protects abusers but drowns victims. Even if Kendie had the strength to do something, she would have needed to scramble for every microphone, fight to hold abusers accountable, crawl to move upward against the empire of the powerful who cling to their crowns on elevated thrones. The villain here is the stonewalling, the shrugs, the constant smog of *disbelief.* Psychiatrist and professor Dr. Judith Lewis Herman gives us a reason why this happens: "It is very tempting to take the side of the perpetrator. All the perpetrator asks is that the bystander do nothing."[3]

What I find deeply tragic is that Kendie has still asked for a chaplain. Someone religious. Some part of her *still* wants to connect to the thing she trusted. Part of her grief is from holding on to the truth, before it was gnarled into a lie.

I notice tears sting my eyes, burn, catch fire. I am angry for Kendie. I have seen many patients like her, but there is a look, an echo, a current that arcs from her voice to an exposed nerve in me. I feel her story through my teeth. Something else too: My brainfolds are brushed with the harsh tongue of some word I cannot understand, but my chest knows what it is, my stomach is a kiln with a closed door but I smell the fumes. I sense something ancient passing through me, a river eons old, caught in the looping wave of a story that has been told for us. The crest of this wave is a closed fist; I have seen this surge pierce through offspring, a rage inherited. *Caught in a cycle, a violent lineage, am I doomed to pass this on?* I have an image of a child, I don't know who—*Is this me? Is this you?*—and when my anger wants to stand me to my feet, my tendons melt between my joints, a sweeping exhaustion pulling every volt of power from me, and I have an urge to put my hands over my eyes, as if to blot out the light. I feel anger, but fear too. A languishing. I almost find this child through the smoke, but then I am pulled back to my patient when she says—

"No one, not one person believes me."

For a moment, though I shouldn't, I remove part of my mask. For just three words.

"I believe you."

Maybe I shouldn't have said it. Part of clinical training in the mental health field teaches to be wary of self-disclosure. In other words, don't compare, don't story-top, keep a professional distance, make sure to center the patient. I get that. I get that swapping stories isn't really my role; it can throw off the dynamic, it can "diminish the authority" of the provider.

But once in a while, I sense a world of overlap, and I self-disclose. I share a glimpse of myself to honor the glimpse my patient has shared. *I went through it too. I'm with you in it.* I'm reminded of these words: "If stories come to you, care for them. And learn to give them away where they are needed."[4] So this time, I share. About being abused as a child. About what it has done to me, what it has told me. I tell her that I know it's not the same, that my sharing is not enough. She weeps with me anyway. I haven't walked in her shoes, not even close, but I sense our footsteps have long and deep tracks, the times we had to carry ourselves through hell.

For a while, after exchanging stories, we are silent. This sort of moment is rare, when two voices have spoken and have been heard in the space of a low-ceiling room that now feels miles tall, expanded. Two voices connecting, I have found, is sometimes all it takes for those two voices to leave differently, to leave whole. A part of me is shaken by this encounter, shaken by her story, and another part of me recognizes we have really met, even just as two bruised reeds leaning on each other.

Kendie tells me, in full strength: "Thank you for surviving."

I saw in my patient Kendie what I have seen in many victims of abuse: More than just the burial of her worth under bruises, she had also been persuaded her loss wasn't real. She never had a chance to grieve the person she was before the violence entered and stole her.

If you're like me, you've tried to find a single ear to hear you—but you got rushed to resolution, you were taught romanticized ideas about nuance and backstory and reconciliation, and forgiveness was made a fairy tale. You were told to stay levelheaded, watch your tone, be the stalwart saint, drag yourself up to the moral high ground, take the high road—until you went right off a cliff. You were told that your abuser was really trying and they'd repaid their debt and they'd apologized a million times.

I had done the same sort of thing with another patient myself. While digging an empty can into her thigh, Martina told me her sister would jump on her stomach at night, regularly tried to drown her in the tub, and about once a week, would wait until Martina was asleep and then slip a needle in her ear.

"I've been sick now eleven years," Martina said. "No one can tell me what's wrong. If my sister were here in this bed, I wouldn't blink. I got no sympathy for the devil."

Here's where I made the mistake. Not just a mistake. I took a salt-shaker to my patient's wound. I asked Martina, "So what do you think it would look like to forgive your sister?"

"Oh," she said. "You sound like my pastor. He told me if I don't forgive my sister, then I'll go to hell. You believe that? How are you supposed to forgive the devil anyway?"

I tried again. Made another mistake. "Do you think you've been sick for eleven years because you've held on to what she did?" As soon as I said it, I regretted it. Martina gripped the can tight, and I could see in her face both frustration and exhaustion.

"Chaplain," she said with a sigh, "you ever think I've been sick this long because I was *abused every single day of my childhood and never got a single night of good sleep?*"

Then it happened. My patient shifted under her sheet, shoulders rolled back, neck turned away. Her eyes glazed, went glassy, overcast. From a distance it would have been easy to miss, but up close the body doesn't lie. *The Grand Closing.* I'd lost my patient's attention, her trust, her chance. I was more of the same, one more guy safely peering off a ship deck in a roiling sea of voices, asking her, "*Have you tried swimming yet?*" I opened my mouth to say something else—but I knew that even if right then I had sung the most poetic combination of words, they would have only seared like acid.

I wondered how many times this had happened to Martina. How many times has it happened to you? How many times has someone spoken circles around your pain, like I just had hers, even labeling your anger more offensive than the abuse itself? This inability to *listen and believe* was not only dismissal but also fear, avoidance, a self-soothing ignorance. It became clear to me that all our reflexes to deny expressions of grief are also the very same reflexes that diminish how to hear victims of abuse. And in a victim's situation, this is terminal.

I had strolled in with the trite placebo of *Let Go of Your Hate and Love Will Change Things*, but it was simplistic and anemic in the face of the evil perpetrated. I was preaching a false version of forgiveness, forced on victims, stealing the air from the room. The only prescription I knew for my patient's wound was to pretend us past it, a placebo, as good as pouring glue in her gash.

Maybe you've heard the same false prescriptions, offered in all sincerity, and you felt a sudden and interminable distance between you and any relief, and you were sure any movement you made would be interpreted as self-pitying, uncivil, grabbing for limelight.

Along the way, your story of abuse was deferred to the abuser, made a footnote, distorted, deflected, labeled everything else except a loss.

But as with any grief, your story has to be told. The person you were might have been buried, but is still gasping for sun, for a hearing, for restitution.

I remember early on in my chaplain training, during a reflection time, I told my story of childhood abuse to my group. I was laughing about it a bit—I'm a son of immigrants, what did my parents know, we all grew up that way, my baggage was a badge of credibility, I joked. And Alisha, one of the chaplains, kept telling me, "What happened to you was not okay." She wasn't smiling. I said it was okay, but she kept repeating, "What happened to you was not okay." And I kept laughing, and she kept saying it over and over, "It was not okay," and I was still laughing but tears ran down my face, down my marked and tired body. I didn't know it, I didn't want to know it. But my body knew. It was the first time anybody had named it for me. It was not okay. I needed someone else to say it. To believe it.

Maybe this is the first time you've heard it too.

What happened to you was not okay.

I'm sorry. If they never said sorry, if nobody ever heard your side of the story.

I'm sorry. They should've been sorry. It was not okay.

If there's only one thing I can do while we're here, it's to remind you—your dignity might have been refused, but it can't be removed. The abuse may have buried you, but there was no loss of your worth. You are still woven tightly with the golden thread of your value. I believe, have to believe, this is still possible to unearth.

## A TREASURE HUNT: UNBURYING THIS GOLD

*You can't be too hard on people. They only*
*know the world they came from.*

— ADVICE FROM AN UNHOUSED PATIENT

Becoming a parent, I knew this: I did not want to pass on the pain I had absorbed.

But I had to wonder: How would I even begin to untether the abuse of my body from my own worth as a human? It seemed inextricable. The scars touched deep. Embedded in deep recesses, in reflexes, in depths I couldn't see.

It became clear in startling moments, a door closing, a shout down the street, the way someone stood too close. Or when somebody gave me a compliment and I assumed it to be sarcasm. I attached to harsh feedback instead, because it verified my false narrative that something was really sick in me. My baseline was that nothing good lived here, not in this shorn vessel. Anybody who'd ever seen wrong in me had to be right.

How was I supposed to override a narrative like that? I was already overridden. I was an essay with pre-scratched red ink, as red as the scar tissue that never dissolved.

I had learned in chaplaincy about *trauma*. It was defined as the imprint left by a harmful event that outweighs our resources to cope with it.[5] It's been said that *epigenetic trauma* gets passed on to our children, either by blood or by bedtime stories. Either way, our genes are marked. Those of us descended from the enslaved, the imprisoned, disaster survivors, or abusive parents—we carry their bones.[6]

We are all given the chance to change this, to pass on something else. In this remains a choice we never should have to make: *How will I suture this wound, that I would not pass on such pain, but something better instead?*

I am in the first year of marriage when I enter the chaplaincy program, which compels me to do internal work at warp speed. It's a hyperbaric therapy chamber. I get to confront my grief, my faith, my family of origin, and all those ACEs (adverse childhood experiences).[7] But after my daughter is born, many of my brain scars resurface. After my wife's PPD, I begin to see a therapist and to take medication. But that barely opens the roads; the highways are still bent and busted. I need deeper work.

After my daughter's 돌잔치 (doljanchi: one-year celebration), I find a trauma therapist, Sheryle. Sheryle had done a seminar for the chaplains. I ask her about therapy and she thinks I can get covered by a grant through VOCA, the Victims of Crime Act, if I suffered abuse as a child. I tell her flashes of my childhood. Bloody nose, scar on my head, struck in the face repeatedly, beaten with nunchucks. Actual wooden nunchucks—and Sheryle stops me. I qualify for the grant. It's a tragic thing that I qualify. But I am thankful, too, that in a system so opaque and obdurate, there is a small hand to help in excavating all I lost.

Sheryle asks me to name some things I believe because of my trauma.

I immediately tell her, "That's an easy one. Nobody's in my corner. No one sees me. I am helpless. I feel helpless to change what happened."

"What do you wish to change?"

"I wanted to stop my parents," I tell her. "I was too small. I mean, wouldn't they have stopped someone from beating up a kid? I wish I could've stepped in there. For myself."

"Someone in your corner."

"Yes. Instead I was cornered. And sometimes I get this . . . this rage. But it's an exhausting rage. Like those underwater dreams when your arms won't lift. I remember that feeling of being helpless. I just took it and took it. But the whole time I was just stockpiling all the violence; I feel it in my veins. They put rage in my chest. Packed it tight into these explosives, tiny pipe bombs, that are just sitting in my sternum. I don't want to pass this on. I have to defuse these chest bombs. I mean, I'm sure you've heard this before, but I would never—"

Sheryle interrupts me. It is gentle, but she is quick to the cut. What she says next is the first time I've heard anyone say it.

"I've been doing this for forty years. I've heard that one a lot: 'I would never hurt my wife. I would never hurt my kids.' I'm sure you'd never choose to hurt them. But people with trauma respond out of trauma. I'm not blaming them. But they couldn't get the help. Couldn't work on themselves. So I wouldn't *say* never. You're here so it can *be* never."

We pause. I expect her to say one more sentence, to end on a softer note. She doesn't. I imagine everything she's seen in forty years. I remember what I've seen in my almost-decade as a chaplain. I see both her resolve and resignation. She cannot, and will not, coddle me. Part of me is relieved at this, honestly. Because I learn that destructive anger doesn't always look that much different from wounded anger. The reasons, for sure, are worlds apart. But the results are close enough to be two hands of the same body. Or as author and educator Layla F. Saad says, "There's a fine line between rage that empowers, and rage that devours."[8] And even if I never intentionally set out to manipulate my family, even if I never for a second have an abusive thought toward them—my trauma could still emerge as a *trauma response*, a coping mechanism to protect myself. It could still harm them. It's how at least some abusers come to be who they are. Our justified anger at abuse can become abusive anger. And I don't want that.

But I'm nervous about all this. I agree with Sheryle, mostly, but—I am still certain my anger is part of me. What if anger is our bodies resisting a brutal world? When I am wronged, I believe my anger is right. I trust it. What is the clear line between destructive anger and righteous anger? Because I've seen patients labeled as *aggressive* or *noncompliant*, when really they were upset because their very valid needs were not being met.

I've validated over and over the rage of my harmed patients, the ones who have faced abuse and bigotry and abandonment and all the ways their communities have failed them. I've validated their rage at God. I'm often the first clergy, even the first person, who has ever told them their anger is good, is necessary.

*My anger is part of me,* I keep thinking, part of my great-grandfather, Park Hee Rak, who was one of the lead revolutionaries of three thousand freedom fighters against the Empire. This anger is part of my mother and father, who even as they were violent at home, protected themselves in a land unkind to them, speaking up when spoken down to.

I tell Sheryle, clutching my chest, "This anger . . . is a fire I want to keep. It moves me out of being passive. Motivates me to burn down bad systems. Sends me to stick up for wounded people. It's good and it's right, I think. Maybe it's what makes me a chaplain."

"I don't disagree," Sheryle says, her eyes warm. "So is your trauma keeping you from acting on your anger in the best way?"

I consider this. "I think so." I find myself nodding. "Maybe the trauma inside is like lighter fluid. I guess I never learned how to hold my story without it burning me. That's probably where I'm at. I don't want it to burn my family."

A couple months after talk therapy, after Sheryle and I have built a bridge of rapport, she walks me through our first session of EMDR—Eye Movement Desensitization and Reprocessing. You may have heard of it; it's almost a hand-eye coordination game while taking a stroll down trauma lane. It's meant to treat PTSD, and like any modality of treatment, the results can vary.

I have my doubts. My old atheism roots keep me skeptical. But I also have the thought, *Maybe I'm one of those guys who will immediately fall into a trance and spontaneously play the clarinet.*

Since Sheryle and I are meeting virtually, I am to follow the movement of her fingers with my eyes through the webcam. I am to think on the word that I used: *helpless.*

"Okay," I tell Sheryle. "I'm ready."

Sheryle moves her fingers left and right. Fifteen seconds. Then she asks me to close my eyes. She says, "When you're ready, tell me what comes up for you. Tell me what you see."

And—what I see next is so immediate, so visceral, I almost slip off my chair. A window opens between my lobes, and a draft enters.

A flashback, vivid and painful. This is apparently rare in the middle of an EMDR session. I'm one of the lucky susceptible few. I'm overwhelmed by a near-hallucination, and it's so colorful, so vibrant, I can barely keep up with describing it, like I'm reading passing graffiti from a subway train.

*I am five. My mother has caught my father in his affair. My mother is holding the woman at gunpoint. The police enter. My mother drops the gun. The officers handcuff her. The handcuffs are loud. I run to the door. A fog of red and blue. I try to open the door. To chase her. I try. I want to yell: "Take me instead. Please take me. Please not her. Take me."*

*Something changes in my memory. I make the change. This time, I run out the door. I run to my mother. She turns and I see her. I am afraid. Afraid of her. But I see her. I really see her. Her war. Her poverty. Her hunger. Her father, who died drunk in a puddle two inches deep. Her mother, who stalked her with glowing metal tongs, to burn the bad out of her. Her sisters, her brother, mental illness their only companion. My mother, bruises under eyes, my father's fists not far behind.*

*I see my father. I want to be angry. But I see his dirt-floor home. Planes overhead. My father is ten. His mother covers his body and those of his five siblings. Bombs falling from the sky. They call this the Forgotten War. My father and violence. His parents were violent. My great-grandfather. In a cell for four years, fighting for us. Beaten unrecognizable. They used their own bodies to cover their children.*

*My mother and father—their bodies are covering me.*

*And then I see—I am covering my mother. I am covering my father.*

*I see my parents as children. Who they were before the world entered. In my chest, there is the anger. But it is merging, filling, rounded out by more. In it, there is grief. Grief for the people they used to be. I grieve that I never got to meet the whole versions of them, before the world stole so much from them.*

I open my eyes. My temples are pounding. I have this sensation that I was somewhere else for a long time. Then Sheryle asks me, "Can you name a recent time when you felt safe? Yourself? Completely relaxed?"

"Yes," I tell her, blinking sweat. "I danced with my daughter. She started walking recently. Now she's dancing. We danced to 'September' by Earth, Wind & Fire. Her favorite song."

"We're going to do the eye movement again," Sheryle says. "Close your eyes. Then when you're ready, you can tell me what you saw. And one more thing. *Let your daughter be your teacher.*"

I follow her fingers again. I think about my daughter dancing.

And I feel the draft again. *I am in a hospital room. It is dark. A welcoming dark. I enter slowly, like I do in every patient's room, as gently as possible. I see my patient. His bed is in the far corner. He is ten years old. He is me. I expect to see a scared and timid child, bruised and shaking, awkward elbows and ankles, the mushroom haircut below the eyeline.*

*But he's not scared. He throws off the blanket and he stands up on the bed. He jumps up and down, laughing. The room is still dark but I can see him, I can see me, dancing in circles. I remember this kid. I remember him. What it was like. Safe. Those rare moments I was safe enough to be me.*

*He waves at me. Waves for me to join him.*

*I take a step closer. Does he know what's going to happen? I step again. Does he know what the world will make him? I wish I could protect him from everything that's coming. But how do you protect yourself when you don't have the power yet? I was supposed to have been kept safe.*

*"I'm sorry," I tell him. "I can't change what happened to us."*

*I reach out my hands. I'm in the corner now with him, with me. He grabs my hands and pulls me up with him. He is so strong. He just lifts me. I stand there. He's still jumping up and down. I have a flash of my daughter, both of us holding hands, dancing, laughing. "I remember," I tell him. "I remember this. I remember you."*

*He says, "Okay! Good! Okay!"*

*For a moment, I look behind me. It's not lost on me that he's in the corner and I am with him. I am in his corner.*

*"Good!" he says again. "Good!"*

*Before I open my eyes, the very moment before I return, I almost move to dance.*

*I am ten. I remember.*

I miss that kid. He was a good kid, I think. He didn't have a lot of time to be himself. But still, he had some time, before time took him, before the world moved in. I wonder what he would think of us, all grown-up. I'd like to tell him that my anger was protecting him. It was a good thing, really. But I forgot what it was like to be that kid. I grieve him. I grieve how I used to dance like that. With no embarrassment. It was good. I had laughed as loud as I wanted to.

I grieve what my trauma has taken—but in that grief, I'm able to remember who he was. Who I was. In grief, there is this: We can reconcile with what was buried and banished, the parts of us that never had a chance to dance.

I open my eyes. Sheryle asks me what I saw.

"What I saw," I tell her, eyes full, "is that they couldn't take everything."

My mother does not meet my daughter until her second birthday. My mother and I have a history pockmarked with half-reconciliations.

She'd explode, she'd apologize, I'd come back. But in my wife's second trimester, my mother had exploded on us in a restaurant. On my birthday. That was when I decided: *I'm not going back.*

Then a few months before my daughter turns two, I have built up some emotional reservoir through trauma therapy, enough to soften to the idea of my daughter meeting my mother. They meet at my daughter's second birthday party. The entire time, I wait, I worry. But I am relieved: It goes well.

A few months later, my mother is in our home, playing with my daughter. At one point my daughter screams because her doll falls over. I tell her it's okay to cry. Then I squat down to her eye level and say, "If your head feels hot, do you remember what we do?" My daughter says, "Breathe." She inhales a big gulp, then breathes out slowly. We pick up her doll together.

At another point my daughter slips and falls. She cries. I pick her up. I tell her again, "It's okay to cry." She tells me, "I cry. Dada says it's okay to cry." During lunch my daughter wants to stop eating midmeal and dance. We pause eating, turn on music, and dance. Two songs later, we keep eating. We pick out some clothes and I ask my daughter, "This one or this one?" She tells me she doesn't like either one. I pick two more. "This one or this one?" We go through about twelve outfits. She finds one she likes. None of it matches. She loves it. So do I.

With each thing I do, there's a refrain. Every time I interact with my daughter, my mother asks me, "Where did you learn that?" Each time, I'm not sure how to answer.

"I never did any of this," she finally says. "I didn't even ask you questions."

"Oh. That's okay, Mom."

"Listen," she says. "I didn't know. I'm surprised at you. I don't think you could do this. So, really, where did you learn all this? Reading books or something?"

I shrug. "I'm not sure, Mom. I tried reading some books but they didn't work."

"So where? You just make it up?"

I am tense. "Mom. I don't know. But it's not from—"

I almost say it: *you.* Then she makes this face. She knows what I want to say. And I see the quickest flash of weariness. A guilt. I can see one lip moving. She is upset. But I don't think it's at me. At herself, maybe. I am still tense, but my shoulders drop a bit. I know she didn't get what she needed. No one showed her. *Who was in her corner?* And I see now, her surprise is real. She is surprised at seeing me, her child, be a father.

I am, I realize, holding a blade between us. I could easily move it in her direction. It is a blade she has used against me often enough. Until it became mine, until my pain became a way to defend myself. It is exhausting. Faced with monsters all day, what else can we do?

But the look on my mother's face: I have met monsters, and I am not sure she is still one of them. I wonder now if she needed this blade to keep herself safe too. I wonder, if after all this time, she has never had a second to set it down.

*How long must I hold this blade?* I have asked myself, just as I'm sure you have asked yourself. Awhile, I bet. It's needed, too often. Then I see you, and you see me, and so many of us are children clutching these weapons, and we never learned to be safe without them.

I'm remembering a patient who was breathing his last and his daughter had thrown herself on his body. They had been estranged for years. The only safe way for his daughter to visit was when her father was dying. She was screaming in her father's ear. I only caught these two phrases, repeated over and over: "I hate you" and "I'm here."

She was angry; it was justified. And threaded through her anger was something else. A grief, an ache for more. A need for her father to have been someone better. I think she grieved for herself, the ways she had been haunted by this ancient specter of violence, a shadow that had been inherited through an uninterrupted sieve.

She didn't have to be there. Anyone would understand if she had never taken that flight. Many don't make the trip. You don't have to either. Still, she was in the room. As if to defy the room, refusing to be bound by its confines.

I have seen this story repeated at deathbeds: estranged adult children visiting a final time, seeing if their parents can finally acknowledge their own wrong with just a nod, the shape of an apology. Layers of rage and injuries, shifting sediments and fractures, hoping that closure might emerge from death before the casket is closed.

Here is what I mean to tell you. In one hand, my patient's daughter held anger. *I hate you.* It made sense. She had been desecrated by her father. In her other hand, she held this strength: *I'm here.* She did not allow his desecration to desecrate how she saw her father or herself. It is not a strength she ever should have needed. But she found it. In one hand, she gripped a necessary scale of justice. In the other, she held, and was held by, a grace that wanted to understand.

I think, if I can put it this way, she had made this choice, one made over and over: *After you have wounded me, I make a choice to keep my humanity by seeing yours.*

I consider this choice as a means not to exonerate but to see. A choice that can be made at a deathbed, or after death, or across town, across the planet, across a lifetime. To be sure, I'm uneasy with the idea of backstorying my abuser; it seems too simple; I cannot prescribe this for all of my patients. But I think it's more than this. I remember those children who screamed at their fathers and mothers, both "I hate you" and "I'm here," and this is a sort of grace on fire. Not forgetting or a forced reunion. Not closing our eyes to what our abusers have done—but more like grieving what they might have become. A grief overflowing with anger and sorrow and a hard compassion. We grieve the people they should've been, and in some small way, maybe this is part of forgiving them. Not the counterfeit version of forgiveness peddled by abusers to absolve themselves. Not permission to enable our abusers. It is permission to be angry at what we lost and permission to grieve a dream of what can never be.

I consider the image I had seen in therapy. Of my parents covering me. Of how I covered them. It tells me: *What abuse has buried, grace can cover.* I am a shorn vessel, but at the deepest core I am still gold, and this treasure will be my child's inheritance. I consider how grace can disrupt a seemingly inevitable story of old wounds so that our injuries do not become portals to pass on pain but to pass on the most whole parts of ourselves instead. How grace reminds us we are bearers of a permanent and irrevocable worth. I consider, briefly, if this is what it means to be covered by the very grace of God.

I imagine how God must witness all this violence in secret corners, in hospital beds, in headlines, seeping through policy and indifference. I imagine God grieving how our hands would be used for anything other than holding, the anger and sorrow that God must hold for each of us who are lied to about our dignity. If I could see, even just a glimpse as God sees, then I would know that I have the right to be angry, to weep for what might have been, and I could set down this weapon so I could walk away free.

I pause. I reconsider myself. I look at my daughter. She is in the corner dancing.

I look into my daughter's face. There is some of me. Some of my wife. And all those before me. My mother too. But there is also something else. Something that is my daughter's own. More. Real possibility. A world fully open. Unmapped joy. Before the world enters. Before voices tell her otherwise. I hope to God she keeps this. The dancing. The fire. I hope she keeps enough of herself, so that in each room she enters she will feel at home, because home is her own body and she will be safe there, safe enough to dance in her golden skin.

Under that golden skin, through the flow of black hair, behind crescent eyes, is a line of those behind her, always behind her—and ahead, further, always with her, beside her, to remind her: *You were always all we dreamed.*

There is no guarantee that telling her about her worth will proof her against the harshness of the world. A simple cognitive suggestion in her ear cannot change granite systems set against her. Even those who know their own value get stuck in bad places. I can only hope that the trace of my voice, a simple echo, will remain. A nucleus of strength. That she remembers a whisper of her worth from a memory of her father along the shore of this ceaseless ocean. And if so, she may find herself. If there is a chance, just one—I will keep reminding her. *You are worth more. If you forget me, please do not forget this: You are always worth more.*

With music or silence, in company and alone, I hope that in her corner she can be herself, and that always I will be there, legs moving in rhythm, and she will know I am for her.

"So, really, where did you learn all this?" my mother asks.

I remember the words of my therapist—*Let your daughter be your teacher*—and this is how I want to answer my mother: *I am learning from my daughter.* When I see her, I know this is true. She is teaching me. But the weight of these words also feels like a burden on her, another unfairness on our children who already enter an impartial world.

My daughter *is* teaching me. And she is also reminding me. She reminds me of when I was unencumbered. She moves me. She has moved me to reach into my own guts to cut the cycle; I have done this work to exorcise old demons, to un-haunt the room.

For now, I can only answer my mother:

"I think I learned it from her."

We both see my daughter dancing. My mom and I can't help but laugh.

*Part Three*

# LOSING BODY

*five*

# LOSS OF AUTONOMY: MOST OF ALL YOUR SELF

On losing our ability and choice,
and what we can still choose.

*Ne te quaesiveris extra.*[1]

—LATIN PHRASE WHICH MEANS, "DO NOT SEEK OUTSIDE
YOURSELF." AN ADAGE TO MOVE INDIVIDUALLY.

백지장도 맞들면 낫다.

—KOREAN IDIOM WHICH TRANSLATES TO "BETTER
TO LIFT IT TOGETHER, EVEN JUST A SHEET OF
PAPER." AN ADAGE TO MOVE COMMUNALLY.

I visited Mayzie five times before he died.

Christopher Mason Hampton, or as he preferred to be called, Mayzie, tells me he won't make it out of his forties. His sickle cell anemia smuggles in chronic pain, neuropathy, and paresis that occasionally turns into paralysis. Eventually, he's supposed to die of a stroke or liver failure or ACS, acute chest syndrome, a vascular occlusion in the lungs in which he would essentially drown on his red blood cells.

Mayzie only has one emergency contact, his sister, Raneeta. They've been estranged for two years. He's married but separated. Mayzie is told if he ever ends up in a situation where he can't make decisions—unconscious, in surgery, altered mental status—then by proxy law, his wife would automatically be designated as proxy, his decision-maker. Mayzie could designate a healthcare surrogate, anyone he wants to choose. But Mayzie holds off. For him it's less about who and more about why. "I'm not about to make it that real," he says to me later. "I sign that and I'm speaking death over me, you get me?"

It doesn't make sense to me at the time. But Mayzie teaches me that autonomy, the sovereign right to our own body and boundaries, doesn't look the way I thought it did. Part of my role is to advocate for the autonomy of my patients, always informing them that they have the power to decide their own care. So long as they have capacity, I remind them of their power to choose. I had thought autonomy was an inherent right, birthed of individual will, a boundary wrapped in skin.

All those things, I believe, are still true. What I had not accounted for was that my view of autonomy was a flat and theoretical abstract, a cover that only fit a textbook. My framing needed to change. Each of my patients has their own ideas about autonomy and what it means to them. One patient may want the chemotherapy for a chance at six months, another may decide on no chemo, one more month of life without debilitating nausea. One patient may want the transplant, another may be done with the waiting and needles and tests. One patient may plan out every step of their own care, another may place their life in the hands of someone who decides it all. Not everybody wants the shocks and compressions. Not everybody wants the prosthesis and physical therapy. Even if one option seems to grant more autonomy, two patients with the same condition can have opposing ideas about what works for them.

I used to ask this question, one way or another, about a patient's care: *What do you prefer?* But that question soon included another one: *What would help you to feel most autonomous, most yourself?*

From Mayzie, I learn this: *Our autonomy never exists in an isolated vacuum, but is formed by a complexity of values, voices, histories, preferences, and community.*

These boundaries, as much as they can be chosen, are also bound by an unforgiving system. If my patient is disabled, not wealthy, not free of trauma, they have a different set of choices that are never easy, never equitable. They might never get a chance at prosthetics, chemo, a caretaker. Someone like Mayzie, every loss in his body a never-again, has to constantly readjust his life to his own limitations, but more than that, to socially prescribed prejudice and to the brutality of an incomplete system that has no traceable villain except its own bureaucracy.

Our right to an ideal autonomy eventually hits a ceiling. Under that ceiling, I saw all the ways that my patients struggled and strived to be autonomous. Our autonomy is constrained by systemic influences and resources—and still, we look for ways to reside within our own bodies in all the fullness we can.

Mayzie's story was full of turns, secrets, revelations that changed the room. It might not have happened exactly the way I tell it, but if there is anything to catch from the lightning bolt of his life, what Mayzie gave me in his story was this:

*Even as we lose the ability to make decisions,*
*what makes us most dignified*
*is finding the smallest things we can decide.*
*As we grieve the loss of our bodies to wear, tear, and time,*
*we find ways to remain ourselves, as fully as we can, alive.*

## "NOBODY KNOWS THIS PAIN"

The first time I visit Mayzie, he's playing a hospital-issued Nintendo 64. He tells me it's one of the few things that doesn't flare up his joints. I notice his fingers, each one at angles from each other.

"Chaplain? What's good, my guy? Want to play this with me real quick?"

Mayzie pauses the game and smiles big. The sort of smile you'll never forget. Already I know I like him.

"I wish I could. I came by to talk through this form called advance directives. It's optional but we do recommend it. It's got the healthcare surrogate and living will. It's a just-in-case type of thing."

"Dang. It's like that now? Is it *that* bad?"

I see the alarm on Mayzie's face and I stumble through a whole pitch. "Nothing like that, as far as I know. The advance directives forms are standard. I have one, my wife has one, we are each other's healthcare surrogates. But you don't have to do it. It sounds like you've heard of it?"

"They brought that up one time when it was real bad. Like I should start picking my last suit type of bad. You sure I'm good?"

Suddenly, I get the idea to sweat. "Uh, yes, but—"

Mayzie looks at my face and laughs.

"My guy," he says, clutching his stomach, "I'm giving you a hard time. I know I'm fine. I was gonna go longer but you seem like a nice dude."

"I started sweating."

"Trust me, I can see it. I see it."

Then we both laugh. I am always happy about this, that even in crisis, in a hard place like the hospital, we find the entire landscape of being human.

After a beat, I ask Mayzie, "So, how's everything going?"

"I'm ready to be out of here. Making moves, you get me? I'm working on this song. It's a hit. You want to hear it?"

I tell him yes. I want to hear it.

"Oh! Oh, dang. You do. It's not done yet. Everybody in the world is gonna hear this one. You're about to hear a hit."

He holds up his phone. In that instant, I see his smile change. The smallest twitch. He's struggling with his phone. His joints. I have half a mind to help. Mayzie picks up on my movement, the way I was about to lean in to catch him.

"I'm okay, chaplain. I'm okay to do this myself." He sits tall. "I found it, right here. My number one hit right here." It's a recording of himself in the hospital bed. I see the number of views. As if he picks up on this, too, he says, "Yeah, I got like twelve followers. You-know-who did too. That's good company."

The video is two eyes and a nose. No music but his voice, and it's almost a poem.

> *This body don't got me / but my body is not me /*
> *Not just a spot / on my chart / doctor's X-ray /*
> *Got me this paper / not money but loose-leaf*
> *Don't shock me / my mic is all / that my heart needs*

"You like that though?"

"I do," I tell him. "I like that a lot."

"My name is bankable. Amazing Mayzie. It's that easy. And if you—"

His head is thrown back, his knee shoots up. Mayzie puts a hand over his mouth and screams. Then his blanket grows a dark and orange spot, a widening circle, his urine filling the bed.

"Mayzie, I'm going to—"

I turn and the nurse enters. He has just been passing by.

"I can give you some privacy," I tell Mayzie.

"No," he says, eyes closed, sweat pouring. "My guy, can you just hold my hand right quick? Nobody did that in a while, can you do that?"

The nurse administers morphine through the IV. Mayzie's shoulders settle. His face, stretched tight, returns. His hand loosens on mine, but remains.

Mayzie looks over at me and says something I've heard a lot of patients say when they feel they're taking up too much space, too much from the room around them. "That's my bad, chap. You don't have another patient to see?"

"I'm here with you right now," I tell him.

His grip tightens. Almost a handshake. "That's what's up, my guy. I just feel bad."

"Is there a reason you feel bad?"

"I don't like being a charity case."

"I think it's hard for anyone to do this without help."

"Well—I'm always saying 'thank you' but being so grateful all the time is painful. It's wrong. Gratitude shouldn't hurt this much. And it's not just that. When I hurt like this, these episodes—I get different. People try to help me but I'm . . . I can be mean."

"I heard someone tell me once that pain changes people. In a lot of hard ways," I offer.

"That's right on. Like when they say, 'Pain makes you stronger'? Or 'Whatever doesn't kill you makes you stronger'? Nah. I should be the strongest man on earth then. I'm just scared, you get me? Being afraid like that, I'm on edge. Then I get a day off, a little bit of relief, but I know I'll get the pain again. Even when I'm okay, I'm just waiting for when I won't be."

I'm reminded of these words by Audre Lorde from her journal on cancer: "Pain does not mellow you, nor does it ennoble, in my experience. It was hard not to feel pariah, or sometimes too vulnerable to exist."[2]

Mayzie blinks away tears. He hasn't looked away once. He stares deep, sees my tears too. He nods, just a bit, hand squeezing slightly.

I ask him, "Is there—do you have some support back home? Any visitors today?"

"No one right now. I got a sister. But we don't talk. Last I saw her was two Christmases ago. Right after both our parents died. They died in a few months of each other. I got two kids, five and seven. My wife left me when it got to be a lot."

"I'm sorry, Mayzie. That makes me sad to hear, honestly."

"No, no. It's not too bad. I got tired of that feeling, being a burden, you get me? A guy like me never should've tried to have a family. I know that isn't right to say, but who's going to stay for this? The pain all the time. I couldn't play ball with my sons, I couldn't put them on a swing, I can't laugh with them sometimes because it hurts to laugh. They couldn't stand the face I made when I hurt. The *sounds*. I think they got scared of me. I don't hold that against them though. I hold it against me. It's the look on people's faces when they look at me, that's the part that hurts. *Nobody knows this pain*."

There are times like this, when I imagine that I can breathe in deep and take all of this from a patient. I imagine that God hears and bends down through the roof and inhales over our patient, and their every blood cell from lung to ligament finds its shape again, and every part of the pain and fear and disease unravels in a single thread until it is pulled up and out of the body. I can only hold Mayzie's hand. I don't think it's enough. I hate that it's all I can do. And I imagine, for a second, as the world recedes from Mayzie's deteriorating body, something like God's hand covering my hand, covering Mayzie, not a fix, but being with, a steady strand of light that holds.

Mayzie shifts gears. "I'm not ready," he says, pointing to the advance directives paperwork. "You start talking about *The End*, then it shows up."

I have seen this in my patients often: the fear of talking about death, as if somehow death will overhear and slither inside. But I think it's more than this. My patients, especially those with chronic conditions, get tired of losing their now to later. They're exhausted thinking about what *might* happen. It's not that they are looking away from loss. Rather they're already drowning in it all the time.

When you live in loss like that, a constant and abrupt disintegration, the grieving requires a deft and delicate movement. You need the permission to *grieve gently*. What I mean is, if you find that you don't want to talk about it, maybe that's not denial. Maybe you just need awhile to catch up to this loss before the next one.

This is an *anticipatory grief*, the apprehension over loss of the future, a lowering of the sky until there is no sky left. A diagnosis, a debilitating injury, one bad infection, one spot on the scan, five minutes of forgetting a name: You find yourself inside the looming terror of a narrowing tunnel. You peer into mortality and it's shown up early, here for its due. It's a cruel deal. We only get so much time, then that time is spent on saving lost time. You can schedule a whole life down to the second, and it takes a single drop of blood to turn a calendar red.

Grief here is in constant flux, a treatment working only to fail, the surgery a success and then sudden complications, always adjusting to shifting ability, trying to stay ahead on research, inundated with new medical terms, grasping for the memory of the body that once was. Mayzie had said to me, "It's wild the medical stuff you learn when you're sick all the time."

When I bring up these end-of-life decisions, I am, in some sense, tutoring in anticipatory grief. I attempt to guide. This, to me, is not just paperwork. I am attempting to open a window into a dignified death. If this tunnel is collapsing, can I crawl with you then, toward the end?

Because I am drowning in *bad deaths*. I want my patients to catch the overflow of my haunted experience, the regrets of those in their final throes. I am burdened with proxy laws and ventilators and the viciousness of decompensation and I am bursting at every seam with all this terrible knowledge. I have stories. I have hundreds. So there is a desperate part of me, trying to move my patient to this paperwork. I am biased. I enter a situation where the patient never expressed what they wanted and their only family is a handful of half-present strangers guessing what the patient wants, not dignifying them, only preserving themselves. But to impose my will that way, to compel a choice through fear, is against all I am as a chaplain and a companion. So I hold my tongue on all the things I have seen. What do I know, anyway, about each patient in front of me? I can only advise, only step alongside. And in the end, what does my patient have as they lie dying but the space between their voice and their choice?

All I can say is, "Mayzie, I'm concerned."

"My guy, don't be. Last thing I want is to give you any caregiver fatigue." He laughs, shows that big smile again. Then with tears brimming, says to me, "I think I know the answer already, but if possible, could you be my surrogate?"

I am moved by his question. "I wish I could. That's very kind of you to trust me. Is there anyone else you can think of to make those decisions?"

"Yeah," Mayzie says, his hands closing. "My sister. When I'm ready, I'll call her."

# WORTH CONTINGENCY

The next time I see Mayzie, he's in handcuffs. In the Emergency Department. He's in the trauma bay. Stab wound. Self-inflicted. But he has also swung the knife at someone else.

Mayzie enters as a Doe patient. Frenetic Doe.

His bed is angled up nearly ninety degrees. I overhear someone saying his trauma was downgraded from Level 1. It's not as severe as it appeared. There's white sand all over his body. He recognizes me right away. "Chap, hey chap," he says. He raises his hand but forgets about the handcuff. The way it *clinks*, it jars my memory—my mother arrested, her silhouette against a fog of red and blue.

"Chap, let me talk to you. I wasn't trying to hurt anybody. See this?" He points to his stomach. There's a laceration, about two inches. "I did that to myself. But they're cuffing me like this for my safety, they said."

He looks away. Sees the officer walk past. Sees a few of the nurses.

"Chap, can you close this curtain? I don't . . . I don't like being out here like this."

I close the curtain behind us. I ask Mayzie, "Was there a reason you did that to yourself?"

Mayzie tells me this is his annual death wish. About once a year, he tries to find a way to end everything. He tells me it gives him a goal, a finish line, enough to get a sudden strength to walk again, a "bad sort of strength," but it's almost pain relief. This time he has gone to a beach with a knife, to watch the water a final time. But somebody intervened, a crowd gathered, the police were called.

"The pain gets to be too much. It's like my bones are trying to get out of my skin. It's real bad. Real bad in here." He lifts his hand again, *clink*, points up to his temple. "I just . . . I start picturing myself as this blob floating in the clouds. And nobody wants me down there on earth. I'm this worthless blob with a useless body. I'm finished. With everything. I wake up the next day and I ask myself, *Why didn't I die? Why didn't I just die?* I start thinking this is the only thing I can really do." Mayzie pauses a moment, then just almost, a hint of a smile. "Times like this, though, I'm trying to remember what my sister said. She was always saying, 'You did enough today if all you did was today.'"

Mayzie goes on to tell me his sister Raneeta is very involved in *disability justice*, which encompasses not only the physical, but also the social and political.[3] The grief of disability is not only over body, but over a world that assumes equal ability. "The fragility and weakness of my body I can handle," Alice Wong writes. "The fragility of the safety net is something I fear and worry about constantly."[4] Or Meghan O'Rourke on chronic illness: "It took years before I realized that the illness was not just my own; the silence around suffering was our society's pathology."[5] Or Nicole Chung on the systems that fail us: "With our broken safety net, our strained systems of care and support, the deep and corrosive inequalities we have yet to address, it's no wonder that so many of us find ourselves alone, struggling to get the help we need when we or our loved ones are suffering."[6] Mayzie tells me that his sister always reminded him: *Even when we feel like we're not enough, that only makes sense in a system that isn't enough either.*

"I'm sorry you have to be here like this," I tell Mayzie. "You got anything that's giving you strength right now? A good sort of strength?"

"Yeah, chap. I used to have something like that. A few years back before I had to bury my parents, I was playing the keyboard three, four times a week. At my parents' church. Not a lot of folks, but the place was a big old chapel, it made the music sound like a throne room. I was never real big on faith and all that, but you know I can't stay away from music. I'd do some originals some time, like I showed you? My parents were front row every Sunday. My joints were hurting so bad, but I had a reason to be there. Then my dad died. After that, my mom. Then my sister just walked out on me. I tried to keep playing, but my hands, they hurt too bad. My doctor told me that the day was coming when I couldn't play anymore. You think that's a coincidence? I'm not sure it is. I think when you lose the people in the front row of your life, you don't want to make music anymore. But sometimes I think about playing again because I think that will make them come back, like they never left."

Mayzie reaches for my hand, like he did the last time. I hear the *clink* of the handcuff again, and I notice his fingers, gnarled, swollen, spotted with sand. I am hearing two pains: his body that has seemingly failed him, and a system that has certainly failed him. I consider his grief, the loss of his function, the grief of what he used to be able to do. But I think of this other grief, the one set upon him by a standard that never should've been. A traumatic grief that called him *worthless, finished,* that had equated his function with his value. You get that message all the time. You're told the loss of your ability makes you less of a person, unless somehow you become an even better person, a victory story made trophy. *Fight, battle, win,* like any loss is on you. It's anchored by an ingrained point system that measures being a perfectly capable and productive pillar of society. You get told your whole value is in your usefulness, in the minutes you spend busy.

In Korean philosophy, there's an idea called 홍익인간 (Hongik Ingan), the ethic of our benefit to all. Your net worth, according to this principle, is only in what you are contributing. Some parents might even tell their kids, "If you're not making something of your life, you might as well take your life." You've heard this sort of idea pierce through every circle, that we are worth most in our dividends.

You have to know how crushing this is in the hospital. I meet so many patients who can't leave their beds for weeks, for months, in knots because their sum total in supposed human currency appears to be negative, because they're counting all the labor spent on them. The rigid numbers of outcomes, it's a rigged game for hustle and hurry. It doesn't speak to most of us, those living with disease, disability, in disaster, from a bed. *I'm a burden:* I've heard that phrase hundreds of times, tears of guilt, teeth tight, the only thing left for them is the waiting. Do these patients then have no hope? No value apart from performance? Are they still not worth treating, seeing, knowing their names?

I know this. I will never believe our value is contingent on the things we do. And I found this too—we still need something, anything, to know *the soul still feels its worth.* To make the smallest ripple, to have a scrap of agency in a current roaring past us. I think Mayzie has tried to find that somehow, going to a beach with a goal, a tragic and terrible goal, to take back a single locus of control. And I think Mayzie has found it in a keyboard and stained glass, he has found what he was certain was God when he lost himself to chords in a cathedral.

The principle of 홍익인간, even when misapplied, still rings true: We want to feel purposeful. I only wish this purpose was not found in the things we produce. I have to wonder, then, if it is found in the moments we are present for. That we are responsible to just each moment, as far as our voices can reach the end of this tunnel. I wonder how we can see ability as entirely different from autonomy, that we are autonomous not as the result of peak effort, but as the resolve of our convictions.

I reach back for Mayzie's hand. I'm probably not supposed to if he's under arrest. But things like this, this is what a chaplain can do. Tread between the system and the sacred.

"Mayzie, do you ever think about playing piano again?"

"One day, I might. Right now, I'll just do my verses. I can't put music to them yet. I reach for my keyboard at home and I just—I can't see straight. Too much memory. You can't stop memories, even when you want to. You get me?"

We are silent for a moment. Then I ask him if he's written anything new.

"You know it, chap. Would you mind getting my phone from that table? On account of me being cuffed and everything."

On a rolling table nearby, I see his phone, spots of blood on the screen. I sanitize my hands, put on gloves, bring the phone to Mayzie. We hunch over the screen, and through red we watch a dozen of his videos, his verses.

## HOLD THIS STORY SOFTLY

I see Mayzie again four months later. He's asked for me by name. I'm on an overnight shift and it's five in the morning.

"Chap, my guy," Mayzie says. Smile as big as ever. "I'm scheduled for surgery at seven. Taking out my spleen. It's no good anymore. The nurse asked me if I wanted to do that paperwork stuff."

"Yeah? How do you feel about it?"

"Well, I texted Raneeta last night. My sister. I was nervous about the surgery. I asked if I could make her my emergency contact."

I almost jump in about the advance directives, to tell him it would be better to arrange for his sister to be the surrogate. But I hold back a bit. I remind myself that pushing a decision is the quickest way not to get there.

I ask instead, "How do you feel about the surgery now?"

"Truthfully, chap, still nervous. Not my first surgery but it's surgery, you get me? And I didn't think my spleen would go this fast. At least I got an emergency contact now. You proud of me or what?"

He smiles big again. We both laugh.

Right then, a nurse walks in. "Mr. Hampton? Family here for you. Is that okay?"

"Family?" He blinks. "Family?" he asks again.

A young woman enters in a wheelchair. Mayzie almost shouts in laughter. "Raneeta?"

"Mayzie." She puts her face in her hands, only her eyes visible.

For a beat, for several, they stare at each other. I look at each of them. I've been in the room for moments like this one, and always there is a suspended breath. A whole lot to say, not wanting to say it, miles apart and years apart but the entire void of that loss rushing in the room, a hard wind, the sudden ache of time irretrievable. Moments like this, an impasse, I'm never sure if I should be there. But Mayzie says, "Chap, this right here. This. This is my sister. Raneeta." I wonder if, at least this time, I'm supposed to be here.

Mayzie says to Raneeta, "But it's so early though!"

Raneeta laughs through tears. All she can do is weep, is laugh.

Mayzie tells me, "Raneeta, she's—isn't she beautiful like I said?"

I nod yes. This is how I remember Mayzie, how much he is smiling, how happy he is to show me his family.

The surgery is pushed another hour. This is hospital time, a time no one can tell.

Mayzie is back in his bed, Raneeta is sitting close, I'm in a chair at the edge of the bed. Mayzie has asked me to stay for a bit. I get the sense he's not ready to be by himself with his sister yet. Right before he talks again, he gives me a look, one I don't fully grasp until he says the thing that he says.

"Raneeta," he says to his sister, "let me talk to you real quick. I just have to know why you left."

Mayzie's usual smile is gone. He rubs his chin hard, almost angry. "You hurt me, Raneeta. Can you just tell me what it was?"

"I've been wanting to tell you. It just, time got so long. I was embarrassed every week that passed. Is it—it's okay with the chaplain here like this?"

"I prefer that, unless he—unless you need to go." Mayzie gives me a look, one that patients have given me a lot, when they talk with family, or they're surrounded by crowding voices, and all the illness and crisis brings out the hidden tensions and frictions between them, and the look isn't exactly asking me to step in, but almost to say, *"Maybe since you're here, my family won't be so hard on me. You're the buffer. You're a witness to what I've been dealing with."*

I tell Mayzie I'm okay to stay as long as he needs me to.

Raneeta looks at me, then her brother. She talks to both of us. "Dad died, then six weeks later, Mom. It was so quick. It's like I took a nap and woke up and they were gone. With Mom, at least I thought we had a chance, right? Then after that third or fourth code, I told the doctor it was okay to stop. Mom had me be the surrogate, so I was the one who had to decide that. In your mind, maybe deep in there, you thought I had killed Mom. I need to know, Christopher. Do you think that about me? That I killed her?"

Mayzie rubs his chin again. "Truthfully? To be real? A little bit. A little. You know what I wanted."

"Christopher. Mom told me what she wanted. You know what she told me? She said she didn't want to be a burden on you. On me. She asked me to let her go in peace when it got bad. But you know what I did? *I went against her wishes.* I had them do the codes, I had them do everything. I went against Mom. Then I stopped the codes. So I went against you. Do you know the hell I've been living in? Do you know what all of that did to me?"

"Mom said she wanted to go?"

"Mom said she wanted to go. I didn't even want her to. But I saw what they were doing to her body, to try to bring her back. She was right. So I let her be at peace. I had to respect that. *Just like Dad wanted.*" A pause. They look into each other deeply. Raneeta, her voice shaking, says to her brother, "When she asked me to be her voice, *I became her too.* Mom died, and I died."

I see Mayzie soften, his shoulders dropping. "I don't . . . I'm just sorry," Mayzie says.

Raneeta puts a hand over her mouth. Her next words are a whisper through her fingers. "Christopher, I couldn't look at you anymore. You look like Dad sometimes, then Mom sometimes. I didn't leave. I just couldn't stay. I wanted to call you all this time, I wanted to see you. But my . . . my heart, Chris. My baby brother."

Mayzie reaches a hand out. Raneeta grabs his hand in both of hers. No sound but weeping.

Raneeta unclasps one of her hands and holds it open. For me. The same gesture from her brother. The same way, knuckles up and looped thumbs.

The three of us hold this way, one body.

Later that night, I get a call from the nurse. Mayzie's asking me to visit.

This becomes our last interaction.

I get to his room and it's blue, purple, glowing. No light but the moon and ocean through glass. Mayzie points to a chair next to his bed, smiles as big as he can. He's drowsy from the surgery. He tells me his spleen had been almost a pound in weight, about three times the normal size. He's expected to go home the next day, back to the motel; his sister is picking him up in her modified car.

Mayzie takes a breath, puts two bent hands on his stomach. He reaches out his hand again, like he has done on most of our visits, and right then I recognize that it must hurt him to do this, to hold someone's hand, and still he needs it so badly. I hold as gently as I can. Mayzie squeezes my hand in full strength. He winces, but keeps squeezing.

"I only have a short while now," Mayzie says. "You know, you're gonna laugh. You know why I asked to see you? Specifically? You've got the softest hands I've ever held. Anybody ever tell you that? I guess you need some soft hands, if you're holding sad stories all day. But seriously, my guy, what kind of regimen you got for that anyway?"

Mayzie smiles. Then we burst into laughter. I can tell it hurts him. He laughs. With purple and moon streaming in, we laugh, our moment of peace in pain.

## "THE LAST THING HE WANTED"

The final time I see Mayzie, he's with Raneeta. It has been three months.

Mayzie has had a stroke. Hemorrhagic. He's intubated, taken to the Neuroscience ICU. I enter the room and I see Raneeta. She is holding her brother's hand in both of hers.

Raneeta glances at me. "Chaplain, I think this is the one. I don't think he's coming back." After a pause, she tells me, "Last night, he asked me to come by, he had ordered some pizza. I get to his motel and the pizza is at the door. I don't think much of it, I put it on my lap and go inside. He's on the ground. He keeps saying two words over and over, but I don't understand. I had seen him have a stroke once, but this was—I knew it was worse. I called 911, I got off my wheelchair, I stayed next to him on the ground. He just kept looking at me. Trying to smile. He kept saying the two same words, he got quieter and then . . . his eyes went up."

Raneeta was escorted by the ambulance. "Halfway to the hospital, I got what he was trying to say. Two words over and over. He was saying to me, *Mama. Papa. Mama. Papa.*"

Raneeta shows me the paperwork. She tells me that since the last time Mayzie was admitted, he has designated Raneeta as his healthcare surrogate. They even told Mayzie's wife about it. And now Raneeta has to make a decision. The same one she had to make for her mother.

I sit with Raneeta and the palliative team in a consultation room. The meeting is short. The DNR is signed. The rest of the palliative team offer condolences. Then it's just me and Raneeta. She looks at me. "I really have to know this, chaplain. Tell me. Please tell me. Do you think I killed my mom? You've seen all this, right? Years you've been here? What would you have done?"

She leans in close, looking into my face.

I try to think of some neutral response, a chaplain type of answer that will guide her through her own process. It's part of the training: not a solid yes-or-no, not a closing punctuation, but handing her the ellipsis, a move toward her own landing. I have been taught that people with questions often carry their own answers, and the one who listens only lights the way.

But by the look on Raneeta's face, I notice something.

I notice she is really asking for my opinion. And even more than that, I get this thought:

*She's trusting my voice to speak into hers.*

I try to assume that most patients, most people, have it in them to know what's right and true. My job a lot of times as a chaplain, at times as a friend and colleague and parent, is to light a candle and lower it to the floor, in hopes that someone else will find a little more of the path. But I am also certain, more times than we realize, we need hands held to help us along the path itself. Not some roundabout processing, but a definitive and fully cooked meal, a whole reply. At times, I've wondered if the "safe reply" is too safe, and really there is the rare time we need more than an advocate, but a champion. Because in that moment our autonomy has already been stolen by a world of doubt, uncertainty, unknown, uncaring systems, what-ifs, why this, all the ground pulled away, and we ask to borrow just an inch to balance.

This could be a stretch, but in some sense I suppose she is asking me to be her surrogate. Not healthcare, not finances or property—but a refuge of assurance. I wonder if this sort of trust, handing over our sovereignty, however briefly, is how we find safety. *Can you decide this for me? Can I trust you to tell me the right thing? Can I depend on you to be okay? Can you be the good I'm looking for?*

I imagine, as much as I am struggling to come to terms with my faith, that this is like trusting the invisible, the divine, handing ourselves over in our times of woundedness into hands that know these wounds.

I have had to rethink what it really means to land on our own resolve. For sure, I value the individual voice, I advocate the right to our own bodies, the right for each of us to draw the walls of our own sanctuary; there is a danger in groupthink, in the flattening of our voices, in laws stealing our safety. When patients fill out their advance directives, I always remind them that all of this is their own decision: Choose who you want, choose what you want, your care is yours. Medical autonomy is entirely within the right of each individual.

Then I have patients who will not complete the forms unless they first consult with their family. No way around it, they must be in the room together. Usually, it's people of color who insist, *I do nothing without everyone.* Our culture, our tradition, is woven with the communal. My training kicks in and I remind my patient that their family doesn't need to be here to sign the forms. Still, they say, *I won't do it alone.* Not cannot, but *will not.* So I consider: What if my patient deciding collectively *is* their true autonomy? What if, medically and spiritually and culturally, I have been conditioned within a Western grid to think that *My Voice* is the highest peak of importance? What if every voice speaking into mine *is* my voice? What if I am rendered whole not by the volume of my own voice but by the merging of us as an entire waveform, a choir, riverbeds made an ocean?

I have seen this repeatedly: Each of us, without exception, eventually and increasingly loses some measure of autonomy. Age, illness, disability, any number of interruptions in life, will claim your choices. Life unfolds and so do your joints. Time equals grief. The vessel breaks. But I see how severely we are consumed by the grandeur of unilateral self-reliance, a glory grown alone in the desert, the allure of solo endurance. I have seen the false and callous worship of individualism; from it I have seen grow the fatal fruit of bias and disdain against the ill, the elderly, the unhoused, because they are seen as *obstacles burdening my autonomy* instead of *fellow vessels sharing in my autonomy.* You may have felt that disdain for yourself as your organs unraveled and your cells seemingly betrayed you. You may have felt your bodily dependence bumping into the razor edge of independence, the guilt of relying on others while clinging to every shred of your own ability. The irony is that by idolizing a robust autonomy, we shun those deemed to have lost autonomy. Seeking to lean on one another, then, has been shamed, abhorred, anathema.

What I mean to say is that ideally, a lack of autonomy would only be a perceived loss; no one would ever have to fear it because we have always shared in our care, we have always been the shoulder for one another. I have dreamed of an *interdependent care*, braided mutuality, generations giving water and wisdom down the mountain, elders gently relieved of their post, the young shouldering their elders into rest, no soul here expendable, no body discarded at first wear. These places exist but they are as rare as they sound. Still the human heart continues to look for this: the sharing of our grief as time pulls the thread, until our burden is no longer burden, but we find it bearable in each other.

I think, possibly, that Raneeta is looking for this in my answer.

"Raneeta, I—"

I consider her loss. Burying her entire family. Father, mother, brother. I consider their dignity. And hers. I consider the impossible choices she has made. I imagine, when the moment comes, I'd be lucky to have someone like Raneeta by my side. Fighting to see my dignity when I've lost all my ability. To see her own, when no one else would. I see the fullness of tears in her eyes, her trust. I am always thankful for this, when patients lend me their complete selves, which I have done nothing to deserve, but only speaks to how much we need this: another hand to share in the brutal and astonishing experience of being in this body, to dignify the ways we need dignity, to bear the cost of our hardest choices, to plunge in the fullest opening of our guts and story, trusting that this other person would for a moment say, *"I see you and I choose you and I trust you too."*

I gently offer my hand. Enough to notice, but also so she can choose not to reciprocate.

She takes my hand. Knuckles up, looped thumbs.

I tell her, "Raneeta. You did exactly what I would do."

Raneeta is worried her brother won't be able to donate his organs because of his sickle cell anemia. But Mayzie qualifies. He can donate his liver and kidneys. A final thing he wanted to do, the last decision he could make for himself.

I tell Raneeta that we will raise a donor flag the next day in the rose garden, in honor of Mayzie's organ donation. Mayzie's care team also organizes an Honor Walk. The entire team on the unit stands in the hall to honor Mayzie as he is transported to the OR with the surgical team. I consider Raneeta's wheelchair and Mayzie's mobility, and I ask her if it's okay that we're calling this an Honor Walk. Should we call it something else? She thanks me for asking. She only requests that I assist her with her wheelchair.

"It's really okay," she tells me. "The last thing he wanted . . . he wanted to walk without pain. Maybe this is the only way then."

Neuroscience is on the fifth floor, and from the entrance of the unit past two corners are the service elevators that will bring us to the second floor, the OR. A short trip. But the longest one in the world.

We wear "bunny suits," a lot of protective gear, to enter the OR. We sweat almost immediately. Some of the nurses and patient care technicians (PCTs) approach to hug Raneeta. It's shift change, so there are many of the staff along the walls.

Mayzie is taken to the OR. Every life-sustaining measure is removed, and once he reaches natural death, the surgery will begin. The team gives Raneeta every second until the surgery has to start. Raneeta asks me to stay with her. She is holding Mayzie's hand, I am holding Raneeta's hand.

As Mayzie's heart rate drops, Raneeta leans in to her brother's ear. She whispers something. Her eyes run. I can hear just these words:

"Baby boy. You are the most beautiful and I love you forever."

After the service, Raneeta takes me aside and holds up her phone. She says, "This was one of his last videos."

She plays it for me twice. I only see Mayzie's eyes and part of his nose, but I know he's smiling. He starts by saying, "This goes out to my boy, my chaplain. This goes out to you."

It didn't go exactly this way. But as far as I can piece it together, these are Mayzie's words.

*I'm ready for home / but I'd stay another day /*
*if my boy J. was out here to stay /*
*Roll out the red carpet / drumroll / since the start of it /*
*You was always a part of it / you was always at the heart of it /*
*Traversed through the worst of it / but the best part of it /*
*I made a brother / blood and bond / you was my soul surrogate*
*I ain't never forgettin' it / that was the real medicine*
*So long / when I'm all gone /*
*I never rode alone, man*
*You were more than my homeboy /*
*You were always my home, man*

*six*

# LOSS OF HUMANITY: GRIEF, RAGE, AND THE UNMADE

## On the cost of bigotry and what we do with angry grief

Content warning: This chapter contains descriptions of physical violence, racist violence, and transphobic violence. Reader, please be advised.

*Water can only go down the mountain, not up.*

—AN OLD PROVERB THAT MY FATHER REPEATED OFTEN, WHICH
MEANS THAT THOSE WHO ARE "FURTHER UP THE MOUNTAIN"
MUST NOT HOARD THEIR OWN RESOURCES, BUT MUST PASS
DOWN THEIR OWN WISDOM AND AID TO THOSE FURTHER BELOW.

## A GRIEF DENIED: THE BODY PROTESTS

He throws his head into the wall.

He's just heard that his father died.

The deceased is my patient. In the private waiting room, I am with my patient's son and mother. The physician has just broken the news to them: "Your father is dead." This is when my patient's son throws his head into the wall beside me. I move an inch closer to him. He picks up a chair. Throws it on the table. Neither breaks. For a second he looks at the chair. Looks at me, blinks. He throws it again. It doesn't break again. My left eardrum rings. I move closer.

The deceased's mother falls to the floor. Hyperventilates. The physician moves toward her. A Code Purple and a Code Gray are called. Code Purple calls for immediate medical care for an injury. Code Gray is for an "unruly patient or visitor." The Code Purple team enters the small room. Then two security officers enter. The air is hot. The ceiling lowers. The wailing shakes the window.

My patient's son, the man who threw the chair and his head, leaves. Security follows him to the exit. I can hear the man shouting. I see him through the window of the waiting room, pulling at his own hair, scratching his own temples. The Code Purple team takes vitals for my patient's mother, pulse and blood pressure, readying oxygen. Between breaths, she is whispering, "He can't be. He can't." I see her grandson outside on the emergency ramp, screaming his father's name.

He is not allowed to reenter the hospital.

I check on the physician. I check on my patient's mother. I go outside to look for my patient's son. He's already left.

Through the halls, I overhear two types of murmurs. Very familiar. I've heard them before.

The first goes like this:

"You just can't act like that."

"He better not come back here that way."

"Just made it worse on himself."

And the second goes like this, and it's more rare:

"Didn't his dad just die? I'd throw a chair too. They can't just let him be?"

I've lost count of how many times I've been here.

*Your daughter is dead. Your mother died. Your brother didn't make it—*

—followed by shouting, chairs in the air, tables turned, fists and phones thrown.

Around the horror of this news is a tension:

*How much grief is too much? When is our grief too angry? Is there a right way to grieve angry? Who decides what "appropriate" grief is?* And this uncomfortable question under the tongue, a very hushed whisper:

"Would he get to stay if he was white?"

When I protested in the summer of 2020 for Black lives and in the spring of 2021 for Asian lives, a lot of similar questions were posed. *Who decides what is a protest and what is a riot? How much room do we get for anger at injustice? What does justified anger look like in our trauma?*

In hospital hallways, seeing glances, overhearing those murmurs, I notice the two very different types of responses to these questions. In a waiting room, someone would throw a chair, and every time I'd hear the two responses: one saying, "You can't just act like that," the other saying, "I'd throw a chair too." And underneath, I'd see this bias in real time: *The most expressive range of grief, especially in People of Color, is more likely to be seen as aggressive, combative, violent, disruptive.* At entrances, exits, bedsides, deathbeds, I've seen this perception imposed. I've seen it too often for it to be a coincidence.

I've tried to understand it, the disparity.

*Who decides what's too much? And why do they get to decide?*

I process with my fellow chaplain Larry. I bring up the patient's son who was "banned."

"I get why they didn't let him back in," I tell Larry. "What if he would've punched the doctor? Or thrown a chair at somebody? I get it. I want the staff to be safe. Not everybody gets to stay in here. I'm guessing that anyone who's been abused, they'll see that chair flying and get triggered bad. I guess, just—it still bothered me they didn't let him back in. There's a reason that guy was angry."

Larry asks, "Do you think if everybody heard the reason, they'd let him back in?"

"I guess not. That type of outburst is always demonized." Then I can't help but say, "I keep thinking that our waiting rooms should have disposable chairs and bouncy house walls. Just put punching bags in there, or at least some chefs constantly grilling hamburgers."

"Hey, sign me up," Larry says. "I'll be in line for that room."

"Bad News Burgers and Breakable Chairs. That's a whole business."

"I'm serious. Punching bag, a chaplain, pulled pork. That waiting room about to have a wait time."

We laugh a while. Hospital banter. Keeps us alive. Then I process again.

"I can't stop thinking about this one thing. The patient and his family were Black. Maybe I'm reading into it too much. It's—I see the difference when it's a Black family and a white family."

"It could be that. Most people just don't like big emotions. But yeah. I enter every room and I am very aware that I am a large Black man. It shouldn't be a thing. But the bias. That's real. I got this reflex, when I go in a room, I have to drop my shoulders and I have to shrink myself. Or I will be perceived as a threat."

"That's what I call a Race Tax."

Larry laughs. I know this laugh. He shakes his head.

"That's *exactly* what it is."

"I guess I have the opposite problem. I walk in a room and I get seen as a 'foreigner.' I know the look when I see it, they hear *chaplain* and they didn't expect *me*. So I speak English real fast, make a quick pop culture reference, I tell them, 'I promise I work here.' I have to flex myself. Prove that I'm as real as anybody else. If I don't—"

"Then maybe no one will let you in."

"Or no one will let me *back* in."

"Did I ever tell you my theory about why we can't grieve?"

Larry has a lot of theories. I'm always ready for another one. I tell him I'm ready for this one.

"It's like this. Historically, you got oppressive nations taking over smaller ones. Any time you got a bigger nation taking a smaller one, the oppressor is not going to stop to grieve their own dead. They're too busy conquering. If you conquer like that for hundreds of years, then the grieving is just conditioned out of you. The common thing is that most of these oppressive nations happened to be Anglo and Euro, the white Western world. I think they trained themselves out of grief. Then you get to today."

"Not a lot different today," I tell Larry. "Nonstop wheel of achievement, capitalism, hustle and grind. Still a conquest. No time to grieve our losses. We have a case of Westernized grief. Incomplete."

"So if you get a grief that looks 'big,' then that goes against hundreds of years of conditioning. You grieve big, then you're 'not a real man.' No warrior is supposed to cry over their dead."

My brain is racing ahead. "I just thought of this. I imagine the oppressive nation didn't let the subjugated nation grieve either. Subjugated people who get to grieve will eventually retaliate. Because angry grief always moves wounded people to fight back. And the oppressive nation couldn't have that."

"So my Black tears are against the rules. *Be polite, calm down, don't be ungrateful, know your place, take your seat—in the back.* So I code-switch. I shrink myself."

"We're code-switching our whole personalities," I reply.

"Code-switching our grief," Larry agrees.

## TO SEE OURSELVES AS WE WANT TO BE, WE MUST SEE HISTORY AS IT REALLY IS

*Nations reel and stagger on their way; they make hideous mistakes; they commit frightful wrongs; they do great and beautiful things. And shall we not best guide humanity by telling the truth about all this, so far as the truth is ascertainable?*

—W.E.B. DU BOIS, *BLACK RECONSTRUCTION IN AMERICA*[1]

I'm reminded of this: British missionaries in 1807 concocted a "Slave Bible" that omitted chunks of Scripture.[2] In particular, the book of Exodus. Enslavers were afraid these parts of Scripture could inspire and incite rebellion among enslaved Africans. Scripture was not taught as a story, but as a package of precepts imperialized by agenda, baptized into Manifest Destiny, retrofitted to uphold the power of an institution. Theology was stripped of any rising narrative that led to liberation.

The erasure of grief was weaponized to silence the subjugated.

This erasure of grief ensures that no one will challenge the oppressor.

The erasure of grief quells the humanity of the oppressor, so they will not pause to see the humanity of the people they are pillaging.

It worked. Almost.

Despite oppression, oppressed people still found ways to grieve angry.

Spirituals, blues, gospel, jazz, and hip-hop were raw expressions of longing and remembrance in the Black community.

The Indigenous people continued to preserve their heritage in song, dance, art, poetry, storytelling. Around a fire, hair unbraided, many Indigenous communities unravel their pain to hold the burden in many hands.

My own people, the people of Korea, embodied 한 (Han), the "sound of depression which appeals to the heavens, the sound of the nameless and the helpless,"[3] a combination of sorrow, anguish, anger, rage—a hauntedness—for how we have been brutalized, colonized, torn by war, split in half. In all our art and expression, we find ways to remember loss.

Our body has always known: It must express the ways we've been harmed.

In waiting rooms, in wailing, in protests—
our anger is grief given a voice.

## A STRENGTH DESPISED: THE MYTH OF (FORCED) RESILIENCE

*But history always rose to the surface. Among the*
*wreckage, the dead floated to the top.*

—NANCY JOOYOUN KIM, *THE LAST STORY OF MINA LEE*[4]

"Listen to me. I'm not leaving until I get to see him."

Charles's body is in the trauma bay, hands bagged. His body is now evidence. The detective is at bedside. No family allowed.

"You make this happen," Marika yells at the officers. Three security officers are in the hallway outside the trauma bay. She wants in. "You make this happen or I will call every single person I know to get through that door."

Marika is Charles's mother. This is her second son who has been killed. It might become the second time it's called a "justified shooting."

"I'm going to ask," I tell Marika. "I'll find out."

The security officers give me a look. A bit of relief, a bit of *Hope you got the goods on this.*

Marika looks at me for the first time. Up and down. Sees my face. Sees my chaplain badge.

"If anybody can do this," she says, "it's you."

I make my way to the trauma bay. Heartbeat in my bones.

*What do I say, what do I ask, what do I say?*

I enter through the curtain. I see the detective. I see a crime scene investigator taking photos. Flash and click. A lot of blood, more than usual. A lot of plastic on the ground. Syringes, wrappers, gloves, caps, tabs. The code lasted about forty minutes. A code always leaves a mountain of plastic.

I take a look first at Charles. Marika's son. *I have to find some way.* I take a breath.

"Detective, I know this is a big ask but—can Charles have his mother Marika come by? She just wants to say goodbye real fast."

The detective looks at me. Sees my badge. "Hey, chaplain. I can't. Not my call but I can't."

"What if I stayed with her the whole time?"

"Even if it were all of us, I still can't."

I take another breath. The camera flashes, clicks. I get an idea.

"Is it possible for me to take a photo of Charles? At least I can show a picture of him to his family."

"Hmm." The detective looks back. "Hmm," he says again.

"I can delete the photo right after. I know it's an unusual request, I just—"

"No," he says. "It's not unusual. Just take the one."

"I'm sorry I couldn't make it happen," I tell Marika. "They let me get a picture of him for you. It's the most I could do."

Marika and her mother and I are seated in the waiting room, close enough for our knees to touch.

"I want to see it," Marika tells me.

"Before I show you," I say slowly, "I want you to know that he's . . . going to look different from when you last saw him. He's still attached to a lot of equipment. It's okay if you change your mind at any time."

Marika turns to her mother. "Mama, you don't have to look."

"I'm not going to," Marika's mother says. She puts her head in her hands.

Marika rubs her mother's back. Takes a moment. Looks at the ceiling. Then at me.

"Okay," she says. "Show me."

I hold up the phone. Marika leans in close. Her eyes, unblinking, fill with tears. She is fixed, focused. Time goes by. A minute. Or ten. Marika stands up, walks out of the waiting room and into the hallway. She collapses on the floor and wails.

And she tells me five words that I have never forgotten:

*"He should still be here."*

Another chaplain tends to Marika's mother. I'm in the hallway. I sit on the floor with Marika. We sit like this for two hours.

For those two hours, her every other sentence is, "I'm mad enough to die."

In between this, she tells me about her son Charles. What he meant to her, his grandmother, his children. She tells me it's not her first time navigating all of this: the media, the investigation, the accusations against her son—"What was he doing? Why did he resist?"—trying to sort out if a lawsuit is worth it, and even if they win after years of litigation, how little that money would mean in exchange for Charles. "Just like all of us are taken," she says, putting her fist in her hand, saying again, "I'm mad enough to die."

Marika moves her feet to stand. I ask if I can help. She says yes. We stand together.

I tell her, "I'm sorry I couldn't do more."

She puts her hand on my shoulder and nods. "That's how I always feel."

From my patient's mother, I saw an anger she did not want—but it was a righteous rage.

This justified anger, I am sure, is empathic. Empathic anger moves in with the wounded. It seeks others. It seeks all of us, those with less than us. It returns our rights that were stolen.

Destructive anger is entitled. Entitled anger seeks self. Without empathy. It seeks more of more. It holds up its own rights, to keep them, not to share, but for no one else.

Entitled anger is power seeking power. But empathic anger is something no one asked for, now seeking something that never should have been taken.

I know I have held both. But the one without power who is wounded—from this often emerges empathic anger, and I know this anger to be true. Not a pass for everything. But permission to feel anything.

Both of these angers, I have seen, come out of real need. But empathic anger, I believe, is determined to set right. It is held on behalf of others. It sees. This anger, I have to admire. It is seeking repair.

I see my patient's mother, Marika, again; her mother has been admitted for cardiac arrest. Marika is in a waiting room.

She recognizes me, stops me in the hallway, nearly shakes me by the shoulders. "I heard shots," she says. "I know I heard them. I yelled, 'Shots fired.' I'd know that sound anywhere."

Earlier in the day, the Emergency Department was locked down for a few hours. We had an active shooter alert, but it turned out to be a false alarm.

Marika is convinced she had heard the shots. Her eyes: I know this look, the fear. She asks, "Do you believe me? I heard them laughing. They said it was a door slammed shut. That wasn't it. I know that sound. Those were shots. Do you? Believe me?"

I am certain she is suffering PTSD, that her trauma has turned this noise into a nightmare.[5] I imagine her mind sees her son, the open casket, her mother looking away. Another video of a young Black man brutalized. I remember my fellow chaplain Alisha telling me that after seeing so many videos of Black bodies slashed and bruised and weary, after so many false facts and stats, and one more argument thrown at her that "they deserved it, did they comply, what were they doing"— her spirit had deteriorated. And she had the terrible thought: *Maybe they're right. Maybe I'm not human.*

And Marika, almost hanging on my shoulders, is asking me, "Do you believe me?" knowing she heard those shots because she always hears them. In her dreams, in the crash of wakefulness, when walking with her children, when a door closes, when a light turns off, she remembers her son, and she tries to remember him laughing, but his ghost is a still, flat photo. It is a linked fate,[6] the total accumulation of witnessing brutality in faces that look like hers, the overwhelming absorption of this collective grief: *A wounded face that looks like mine is also my wound.* If you have witnessed the wounded body of the one you love, how soon did rage and anguish make a home in your body too?

She has told me, "I'm mad enough to die." I thought somehow this was a type of strength, an anger that galvanized her, a right kind of ferocity. But I see now, as her knees nearly give way, that is an incomplete picture. I'm reminded right then of a patient who told me, "Even the strongest ones get tired."

My mistake was in admiring Marika only for her determination. She is determined, I have no doubt. But I have failed to see she is enduring a situation she never should have been in—her strength is a forced burden, a compulsory assignment. Some of us have gained strength by choice, a luxury in our life's vision, but many of us were strengthened against our will, against a wave that would eventually wear and tear every joint.

Marika is searching my face, to see her own. "Do you believe me?"

"I heard it," I tell her. "I hear it too."

I am told resilience is how we make it through this trauma. I am not always so sure. If you tell me that I can nurture the strength to walk over bladed and burning ground—why do we not pave a new road instead?

As far as I have seen, in my patients and in my community, resilience was fed to us as a mercenary tactic to persuade us to pull up our own bootstraps. *It is all on you, your effort, to overcome.* I grew to hate this word *overcome*. At best, resilience is an opiate, theoretical and industrialized. Trauma is turned into triumphant testimony. But this only makes for a tacit truce: We begin to tolerate the forces that traumatize us, as if God throws us in a fire to make us iron.

None of my trauma, really, made me tough. Only tired.

Here, I forgo forced resilience. My respite is this: Our collective grief gathers a grace-filled village. Resilience for me is not foremost a toughening. It is refuge. Here, pain is our shared language. I receive your injured hand in mine. And we understand that this wound is something we never should have endured. Our strength is not in endurance. Our strength is in the speaking and hearing of what we have endured. Our strength is in the ongoing dismantling of what harms us. Here, my rage is not turned away. Here, resilience is to rest from this brutality, and to resist when I would be defaced. We are joining in an ancient lament. And I believe, must believe, that God laments here, too, a refuge for our rest and rage, our cover in a fire we did not want but do not have to resist alone.

## A GRIEF WE NEVER ASKED FOR: THE LONG COST OF BIGOTRY

A nurse tells me, "That was the longest code I've ever seen."

She's a travel nurse who just had her first shift in the trauma bay.

She tells me that in the previous hospitals she's worked in, she could always tell when a code would go short.

"Homeless, elderly, disabled . . . Black, Asian, Hispanic . . . multiple comorbidities. Those codes never go long. It's like the whole team is asking, 'How long is he worth?' Apparently, less than it takes to chart them."

I have read that for every 10 percent increase of Black primary care physicians in a county, the life expectancy of the Black community there would increase by one month.[7] An extra month with my elders, my siblings, my daughter? A year? Two?

To be unseen is to be unmade. But to see—this saves lives.

These types of situations are difficult to see, but permeate the earth in all its arteries, filling every channel, basin, and mouth. What we call systemic racism is a river poisoned. In tributaries. In our subconscious. The poison is inextricable from our water, from veins, from our names. Many of us were born in the river. Kept submerged, in verbal mercury, drowning in laws laced with arsenic. Therapist and author Resmaa Menakem speaks on how our historical policies and practices result in racialized trauma, which can remain unmetabolized in our bodies. He coins "white-body supremacy" as a trauma response we've inherited that harms every one of us: "This means that no matter what we look like, if we were born and raised in America, white-body supremacy and our adaptations to it are in our blood. Our very bodies house the unhealed dissonance and trauma of our ancestors."[8]

What is called *white supremacy* is not only about white hoods and hateful slogans. It is not blaming any one individual. And it is not merely a cartoonishly evil backroom ideology. It is an ingrained cultural reflex, an arc pressing down on history and humanity, hooked and rooted, through an old guard and old money passed down by those who forged power. Those in power today can continue to look away. The wounded—those like me, like many of my patients—cannot. We inherit the grief of poisoned waters.

How do we remove this poison from the depths? How do we un-pollute centuries and miles of this river? How do we rewrite trauma passed through blood and law and legacy? Even if you give me the antidote of being willing to see, who will un-poison the river itself?

I am grateful when someone steps in. I wish they didn't have to. To step in is to pay a price, too, but my hope is that in some way, this very step is planting a seed that will be the shade of a tree for those after us.

I remember one specific intervention. My patient's nurse, a young Black woman, tells me softly, "AMS. Liver enzymes." Translation: Our patient likely has elevated bilirubin due to liver disease, which can cause altered mental status (AMS).

But the nurse has something else in her eyes. I know the look. Both steel and empathy. Be ready, she's telling me.

My patient sits up. She is jaundiced, eyes bright red. She glances at me and says, "Hey, you, Oriental boy. Where did you get your nose?"

I flinch. My temples tighten. I remind myself, AMS. She's not herself right now. Short-circuit.

"I'm talking to you," my patient says. "Walk over here. I got some cash for you."

I could leave. Or I could ignore this. Or I could directly address it. I'm a professional but I can still throw down.

The nurse leans over. She tells our patient, "You know that's not okay."

Our patient laughs. But the nurse repeats, "Hey, you know that's not okay."

Our patient laughs again, but quieter this time. The nurse keeps repeating herself. A dozen times. "You know that's not okay." Our patient stops laughing. Agrees. "It's not okay. Sorry, I am not myself." She isn't. Liver enzymes or drugs or delirium. "It's okay," I tell her. But inside, I'm not okay.

Later, I find the nurse. She is busy with another patient, but she glances back at me. Through curtains, we see each other. We share a look. She is tired. Almost resigned. It costs labor to step in, to speak. It is labor to remain whole in our bodies.

I whisper, "Thank you."

The nurse nods, smiles. She shakes her head, almost playfully, as if to say, "The audacity." She quickly places one fist on her chest. To me, I read it like this:

*You got me. I got you.*

I wish she never had to step in. I am glad she stepped in.

Between most patient visits, I take a moment to journal some thoughts. Here, I write this.

*When I see your face*
*and it looks like my face*
*and it is brutalized*
*then in some measure*
*I too experience you*
*I too am erased*
*I too am enraged.*

*I only know that dignity refused*
*is never dignity removed.*
*Even souls inside bodies that are broke*
*hold a dignity that no one can revoke.*

## A STRENGTH WE NEVER NEEDED: THE LONG LAMENT

*"Ar scáth a chéile a mhaireann na daoine."*
*"Under the shelter of each other, the people survive."*

—IRISH APHORISM

My supervisor Frida asked me a question at the start of my chaplaincy, a question that set me on a course I am still running:

"How can you bring alive the parts of you that you had to hide?"

I want you to know that if you, too, ever had to hide to get along, to survive, to climb Mount Assimilate, to blend in and build home—that hiding was not harmless. It was radiation eating cells.

I had erased parts of me to settle for part of me.

But partial me is none of me.

What I grieve is believing I was invisible.

Toni Morrison asked, "'Invisible to whom?' Not to me."[9]

We were never invisible, never voiceless, never silent. Only silenced. It was only our pen and microphone that were taken. We reclaim them.

"So what do we do?"

141

In a didactic early on in our chaplaincy training, our educator for the day asks us this question.

The question he asks is a question for all of us.

*So what do we do?*

He tells us the story of Tyra Hunter, a Black transgender woman who was driving to work and was struck by a car in a hit-and-run. Paramedics failed to give care for Tyra's injury after finding she had a penis. They insulted her in earshot of nearly one hundred witnesses, one paramedic saying, "This b–h ain't no girl . . . it's a n––—, he's got a d–." A posthumous medical report concluded Tyra should have had an 86 percent chance of survival had she been administered proper care. When Tyra died, activists marched wearing shirts printed with her face and the words *God's Gift*.[10]

Our educator reveals to us that he is transgender. He tells us, "I've learned that people are conditional. They'll love you up to a point. Our job is to break these conditions."

*So what do we do? Our job is to break these conditions.*

In systems and spirit, conditions have been set up that refuse one another's dignity, one another's existence. When you see another headline, *Asian woman was ___, Black man was ___, children were ___, immigrants were ___, disabled person was ___, transgender woman was ___, mass shooting, mass shooting, mass mass mass*—their pain must be distinctly our pain, because we know the forces of rejection and denial and bigotry that got them there. This is a collective grief. This is our grief.

There has been, I believe, a global trauma. It is what I had recently told a colleague was our global PTSD, or GPTSD. From it, there has emerged a call for protest, rest, lament, all things transformation. Our angry grief needs movement, needs direction. And just as with any grief, it seems easier to deny, suppress, ignore.

But this grief ignored will only further harm. I consider Maya Angelou's words, both comfort and admonition, and she was right: "If I cry, whether you want to admit it or not, you understand that. And if I mourn, you understand. If you are yearning for something, I see that. The truth is we know each other and *we tell ourselves we don't.*"[11]

We are continually dislocated from our collective grief. We are told it was not *really* a hate crime. There's *nothing* we can do about it. This usually *never* happens. These things *always* happen. They brought it on themselves *anyway.*

Each of these tragedies occurred in part because rampant systems made a sweeping effort to remove empathy from one another, in order to become efficient or to maintain control. And the conditions that destroy these lives are also the very conditions that mandate how to grieve them.

Still, the Image of God cannot be erased. To be unseen is not to be invisible. Our dignity is already and always there. And every wound against the Image calls to another in search of mending. We can neither ignore the Image nor the injury.

This grief, our grief, cannot remain neutral. It moves me to you, you to us.

More than once, after I visit a patient, they ask me to see the person in the bed next to them.

"They've been crying at night."

"They told me no one has visited."

"They might not leave this place."

A curtain separates them. But no curtain can really separate us.

We are joined at our hips, our hands, our hopes, our guts.

When the world is on fire, it is a gash through our collective heart.

For my daughter's sake and yours, I shout for a day when we will no longer need heroes or resilience or vigilance to survive, but instead when systems are turned inside out. A day when our bodies are no longer collateral for think pieces, pundits, platforms, and vigils. But for our bodies to carry peace. Not a false truce, but a real *shalom*, to see one another whole.

Until then—*what do we do?*

In the meantime, I cannot wait the whole time. James Baldwin asked, "How much time do you want for your progress?"[12]

Even as I wait for a day when we no longer have to be afraid,

in this grief, rage, and in being unmade,

*I refuse to refuse the refused.*

In all the ways we can, we make visible the ones who were told they were not.

I run to those put in corners, back rows, against the wall. I run to those grieving in this poisoned river. The rage I hold in this grief moves me to restore us, to a justice that will roll with new waters.

I ask as Howard Thurman did, "The masses of men live with their backs constantly against the wall. They are the poor, the disinherited, the dispossessed. What does our religion say to them?"[13]

For me, our faith says, *I refuse to refuse the refused.*


Your story is ~~crazy~~ valid.

Your grief is ~~too much~~ real.

Your voice is ~~too loud~~ needed.

Your story is ~~fake~~ medicine.


I honor you, Bearer of the Image.

144

*Dear daughter,*

*One day you'll read this and you might roll your eyes a little. We'll laugh. They say children end up teaching their parents, and I'm sure you will show me all the things I missed. You will be all the things I couldn't. And more.*

*You will be—you are—brilliant and beautiful.*

*Not because of your talent or appearance. But simply because you are you. Nothing will revoke this.*

*You will learn one day your great-great-grandfather was a revolutionary in an oppressed Korea ruled by the Empire. You will learn your grandfather fought for this country in a misguided war. He made it to see you, his first grandchild, with his own eyes in this country he loves—even if it did not always love him. You will learn your grandmother labored over a small laundromat where the previous owner kept stealing the quarters from the machines every night.*

*Your family's spirit: your spirit.*

*You will learn that I, your father, was regularly spit on, assaulted, and ignored—mostly because of my skin. I have daydreamed of being someone else. I have tried to take my own life, and sometimes I cannot remove all the voices that have lodged as splinters in my heart.*

*When I was very young, just four, I had my first real memory. It was my first day of preschool and my teacher found out that I could not speak English. This teacher put me in the corner all day, chair facing away from the room. I remember the gray wall, my whole world a fog. I remember sobbing to myself. I remember the children playing behind me, saying words I wanted to understand, their tongues scraping against my brainfolds. I do not fully blame this teacher; it was also the vicious system around her that allowed this violence of unseeing me. And I remember my mother picking me up, seeing what had happened, and yelling at the teacher. Your grandmother used every English swear she knew, filled with a righteous rage I have never forgotten. A rage turned against me at times, but in this moment, for me.*

*From that day, we spoke only English at home. In a couple years, I had forgotten my language. Trauma and assimilation left me with a burned tongue.*

*You might inherit my pain, this trauma. What I can also give you is my story. My hands. Being there. And even the shape of my language, when four-year-old me tumbles free, not gone, only sealed behind fear— sometimes I can give you all of myself before the world moved in.*

*I prayed over you in your mother's womb. I was terrified. Scared of parenting, and afraid because you, a Korean American woman, would enter a world that has not caught up to your beauty and brilliance. Seen as an object, a target, a hologram of projected desire instead. This fills me with a haunted rage.*

*I'm sorry. (I will say this a lot.) There is so much I want to protect you from. But I know I can't. It is presumptuous, after all, to assume I am your savior. And I know you will find the strength and spirit you have always had—no matter how the world spins around you. You will change its axis.*

*You will learn our story, a song of deep suffering. You will also find a heritage of celebration, fierce affinity, of moving forth despite all the things that have threatened to take our humanity. As our pain is passed on, so too is our joy. May this be moved from periphery to center. May it not be reward, but a gift as simple as sun and sky.*

*I see you. Hear you. You bear all the room in my heart, where no splinter can reach. And everything you go through, anything you want to be—I will be there too. I love you. Don't forget.*

I visit an elderly patient who has just died. She is in the bereavement room surrounded by a dozen family members.

The room is loud. There is holding, shouting, rocking. At once I notice that several of the family members have their phones out. They are recording all the weeping and wailing.

I have this strange reflex, an urge to tell them they can't record in here.

But I wonder why I should stop them.

I think of how my great-grandfather fought to have his records remain. How his history was nearly burned to ashes with the rest of his village. We are people who archive. In our bones, we resist to remember home.

*If to remember someone is to make them whole, then I have to believe that to love is to remember.*

I ask one of the family members, "Would you like me to record for you?"

He turns, wipes his face, tells me it's okay. I ask him how he is related.

"Our mother," he says. The people in the room appear the same age. The family is of many different ages. But his reply is, *Our mother.*

The family departs. I am the last one out. Someone in the hall asks me, "Are they your family?" I'm not sure if it's staff or a visitor; my face is marked by weeping.

And I can hear in his voice that it's a joke. A racist question.

"Yes," I tell him. "They are family."

# Part Four

# LOSING HEART

# seven

# LOSS OF CONNECTION: LIFTING IN MIST, WE DRIFT

On loneliness, losing your group,
and re-finding community

> Content warning: This chapter contains descriptions of end-of-life care, depression, and suicide. Reader, please be advised.

*Umuntu ngumuntu ngabantu: a Zulu phrase meaning
"a person is a person through other people."*

## AIRWAY INTACT

*You realize the nurse has only asked for your name to see if your airway is intact.*

*You thought the trauma team asked that to humanize you. To connect. A simple question, an essential one: "Can you tell me your name?" But the nurse hears your name and immediately yells out, "Airway intact."*

*They're doing their job. You know that. Just. Well. For that second, it was nice.*

*You're turned on your side. Someone presses near your neck. They ask, "Does this hurt? Yes or no?" They make their way down your back. Seems to be a standard test. No. No. No. They get to the bottom. "Quick pressure here. Does this hurt?" You tell them no. Not physically.*

*Someone in black scrubs enters with a machine on wheels. It has an arm that extends with a big camera at the top. X-rays, they tell you. The tech yells out, "X-ray." The entire team steps away. Minimum distance six feet. You're getting a small dose of radiation, in hopes they can find injuries from the car accident. Every time the team moves away for the X-ray, you feel like you've pushed them away.*

*Lights are bright. C-collar around the neck, a precaution, but it's awful. The trauma bay is hot. Later you find out that they keep the temperature high in case a patient goes into shock; it's to keep the body from dipping into hypothermia.*

*Suddenly, a man in a tie approaches. He is almost on one knee. You can't turn your head much, but you notice his hair first. It gives him a good three inches of extra height. He appears to be Asian, young-ish, moving slowly, deliberately.*

*"James," he says, polite like. Very polite. He's the first one to call you by name. "My name is Joon and I'm one of the chaplains here."*

*A chaplain. So it's bad, you're guessing.*

*"One of my roles," he continues, "is to connect patients with families. Do you have any family or friends that I can call? Anyone on the way?"*

*The way he says this, it sounds like it's a regular part of his job. This helps you relax a little. Maybe it's not so bad. You only know about chaplains from TV shows, and they always show up when someone's counting their days on one hand.*

*"I got no one," you tell him. "No one."*

*"An emergency contact? Anyone at all I can call for you?"*

*"No, sir," you tell him. "I got no one. I'm alone. I'm a lonely guy."*
*You're not even sure why you added that. Just making conversation with*
*the chaplain in the emergency room.*

*"I'm sorry, James. I'm here for you. You are not alone."*

*He sounds genuine. But you tell him, "No, I am not just lonely. I*
*outlived my family, including my children. I have no one. My problem is*
*that I lived too long."*

*You want to tell him you were lucky that you once had people—you*
*had your wife, who made all the plans with her circle of friends. Your*
*children did too. They are gone now, buried, and their circles slowly left.*
*The sight of you reminded them that your wife and children are dead.*
*Your wife's friends tried to call for a while. You almost went out with them*
*a few times. But no. You said no. For a year. Two. Three. They stopped*
*calling. Dust settled on doorknobs, your dinner table, your eyelids.*

*The chaplain opens his mouth to say something, then closes it. You can*
*tell he doesn't feel too good about what he said.*

*"James," he says. "I'm sorry. What I said wasn't helpful. You are—I*
*hear you. You're alone. And lonely. Thank you for telling me that. Can I*
*get you anything? I can stick around as long as I'm able to."*

*"I'm not bothering you or anything?"*

*"Not at all. If you've got the strength, want to tell me how you got*
*here?"*

*"Chaplain. You won't believe me. It's a long story."*

Loneliness is an agonizing hunger. A gnawing emptiness. It is particular, raw, churning. It's more than a single loss, but an ongoing death.
A perpetual deprivation. The grief here is both quicksand and fog: If

you are lonely, you grieve being unseen, but also grieve that you see no one. If what gives us meaning and memory is moving with community in all our highs and lows, then without this, our achievements seem hollow and our setbacks unbearable. If no one sees, no one hears, no one cares, what does living mean?

There is no official diagnosis for *loneliness* in the latest iteration of the *DSM*, the *Diagnostic and Statistical Manual of Mental Disorders*.[1] It's a hard thing, even embarrassing, to admit to your therapist or primary care physician, "I am lonely." To be lonely is in itself lonely.

Is there a solution to this sort of grief? I thought "You are not alone" would be a comfort, only to find it was a cruel reminder, a flame across a burn. I thought it could be as easy as encouraging a lonely person to *go find people*. But this was as helpful as saying, *"Stay strong, it gets better."* I'd get that look, the one that told me I'd missed the mark by a mile: *"Right, why didn't I think of that before everybody left?"*

Loneliness is a fog in which you need to find connection, but you are certain no one sees you, so you remain in the fog. A self-defeating spiral. For some, the underlying causes of loneliness are depression or anxiety or trauma. Or for those like my patient, James, *My problem is that I lived too long*. The result is the same: isolation. Loneliness is a feedback loop, a tightening and incursive spiral that keeps you alone.

What can we say, if anything, to answer this?

I've seen at least two types of loneliness.

One is *relational*, the other *objective*. Both happen for different reasons, requiring very different responses. But what I see, in the loneliest place in the world, is that loneliness is a universal grief. It says nothing wrong about you, but only something right: that we are in need of each other. And what we need from each other is not exactly the thing we've been looking for.

## RELATIONAL LONELINESS: A SEA OF PEOPLE, BUT CLUTCHING A PLANK ALONE

*Your aunt, uncle, and brother are at bedside, doing all the talking.*

*Every time the physician tells you some new information—here are the risks for the procedure, here's the best and worst we can expect, here's another option—your family escalates. Your uncle, especially. He's hardly been there. But he swoops in on these family meetings, thumps his chest, throws his elbows around. You want to believe there's a part of him doing this because he cares, or that this is his grief acting out; that he can't stand seeing you like this. But you realize that in these meetings he can feel like he's in control of something. Now he's saying so much you can't say a thing.*

*The palliative team is five people. One of them is a chaplain. You're not sure why. You're not religious. You know your illness is bad. Possibly terminal. But does a priest have to be in the room? Just seeing his badge makes you nervous. And if there is a God, any god, none of those prayers worked.*

*You've tuned out for a minute. You come back to your aunt yelling something at the physician, louder than just a minute ago. Your aunt is scared. That's all. Your family is scared. But you're scared too. Who's made any room for that?*

*You sense the palliative team is wrapping up. Concluding on your life. What the end will be like. The physician, she's looking right at you. She's being kind. But she can't get past your family. You want to say something. But you're ready for it to be done. To go back to sleep, to let time crawl until the next thing you're tired of waiting for. You feel that void again, that gulf between you and the room. Your family is at bedside, but they might as well be a thousand feet high. You're alone in this. You're in a room full of people, alone.*

*Then the chaplain speaks. His voice is soft. Almost hard to hear. You notice his hair. It's a bit meticulous.*

"*Hey, Jordan. I know it was a lot of information. How are you feeling about all this?*"

*Feeling. Like I want to throw this cannula and this IV and this bed across the room.*

"*I feel fine.*"

"*Honestly,*" the chaplain says, "*I feel overwhelmed and worried hearing all this. I thought maybe you might be feeling the same things too.*"

"*No,*" your uncle says. "*He's not worried, he's our champ. That's our champ.*"

"*I just know,*" the chaplain says, his voice shaking, "*if you were my nephew, I'd be a little out of my mind right now. I'd want to know anything you're feeling. Or questions you had. Or about anything you wanted.*"

"*No,*" your brother says. "*He's——*"

"*Yeah,*" you finally say. "*The doctor talked about intubation. I don't want that. I don't want anything like that.*"

*The nurse practitioner leans close. She asks, "That right, Jordan? No intubation?"*

"*Only if you really have to. But I would not prefer it.*"

*You almost tell them the whole truth. That you don't want resuscitation either. But this has to be the start. You can't say DNR yet. So DNI, do not intubate. So they'll get used to the idea.*

*You realize you're talking to the chaplain. Directly talking to him. And he sees you.*

It is possible to be in a room full of people but feel more lonely than if the room had been empty. It is to be unseen. Unseen, by those close to you, is in some ways worse than having no one see you. There is no simple medication or meditation for that distance.

This is a relational loneliness. It happens even in the deepest of relationships. It's more than any single argument or rejection. It's a mental and emotional anguish caused by continual relational distress. This is how I see it play out at the hospital: Even when I visit a patient who is surrounded by family, at times I see a loneliness that dims the room, until no one can see the other but for a silhouette, unreachable.

I have seen patients sit quietly as family members take center stage, monologizing in Shakespearean pentameters. I have seen parents or siblings or children override my patient's fears and food orders. I have seen my patients trying to advocate for themselves, and the blank gaze of loneliness when they realize no one is in their corner.

Loneliness accumulates by the continual failure to connect—one more difference of opinion, one more disruption of dialogue, one more incongruent response. It happens when advice is given instead of celebration, when there is domineering instead of listening, when there is an interruption, inattention. And these small gestures, missed chances, mismatches, turn a leak into a sunken home. Even when this failure is not intentional, it can build by incremental instances, which widen to an unscalable chasm.

The hospital has a way of surfacing buried tensions, a long-suppressed grudge, or eventually, the room has to talk about the gravity of the prognosis. That critical juncture exposes the tectonic edges of each person, collapsing and pulling away at the fault lines, distinct human wills crashing but retreating to the base of their own I-am-right-ness. Family sit inches apart and withdraw by miles. You can see it, almost hear it happen. The walls rush up. It is then, each person, as lonely as the next, is no closer to understanding the other. Maybe there was never understanding, and it is only in crisis that they see they are on opposite horizons.

In these critical exposures, we can find ourselves continually recoiling from those we thought closest to us, until even partners in the same bed cannot reach through the canyon dug between them. It seems eventually the only option left is to disconnect completely, a full departure.

*You thought this time they'd call, or even visit.*

*But none of them do. Because—*

*You came out a few years ago.*

*Or you told your family you wouldn't take their abuse anymore.*

*Or you stood up to your boss and you were fired, and it turned out your work friends weren't friends.*

*Or you told your church friends you couldn't vote for that man. Some even agreed, but they couldn't leave with you. And some were deceived, even radicalized, and you tried to reach them, but they called you a lost cause.[2]*

*Or you protested for Ahmaud Arbery and Breonna Taylor and George Floyd, for Michelle Go and Vicha Ratanapakdee, for the victims of the Atlanta spa shooting. You said the insurrection was exactly what it was: a horrific attack. And across the dinner table, your family told you what they really thought—that you were a demon.[3]*

*You knew you had to leave them. But you wonder: Would it have been better to lie, if that would've meant you could keep them? Could you lie a little longer, if that meant you could keep the people you liked? Because they weren't all bad. Were they? It would've been easier if they were.*

*Except it wasn't just a difference of opinion. They could never see you fully. Never know you without imposing their agenda of conversion. If you could compartmentalize, look past their bigotry, even their abuse, at least you'd have somebody around.*

*You grieve their presence. You grieve their absence. You grieve the ghosts of the people you thought you knew, who never knew you, but only the nodding version of you that appeared to get along to belong.*

*Is it enough now to be your only companion?*

*You want to say yes. Of course it is.*

*But you see the outline of a full room. The ones who used to be there. Laughing ghosts. You miss the sound. You miss them. Almost. You remember how they filled the room, even if they didn't fill you. Here in an empty room, you are true to yourself. But the walls echo.*

*All of this makes you shake at the edges. You flip tables alone. You dig into the steering wheel. You infinite scroll on your phone, lurking. You binge episodes, imagining talking with these characters, diving into the screen. You can't have silence; there's always music or a podcast or a video on loop. You sit by yourself on lunch break. A mistake at work puts you in a panic, like you'll be caught and displayed. You can sit in a bath for hours, until your teeth grind.*

*You imagine your funeral. Who attends? Who weeps? Who leaves early? You shuffle through a grocery store, café, bookstore, the park, to look at faces. You're in this hospital bed, and with every set of steps at the door you hope to be surprised. A flash of someone you used to know. Or you wait for the physician, for a nurse, for a specialist, for culinary. You hold them with conversation. You tell them more than they asked for. You apologize for talking so much. But you can't stop. You need this. Any face who will look into yours. Even if they're paid to be there. They have to leave. There is a wire, a filament, attached to them as they go. You have hooked your lifeline into them. It becomes thinner until it snaps. That emptiness sets in your chest again. You hate this feeling. A constant itch.*

*"It sounds like you're lonely," the chaplain suddenly says.*

*Lonely. It's a dramatic thing to say. Too big but too small. Depressed? Anxious? Fatigued? Irritable? Yes. But lonely? Maybe that's it.*

*"Maybe that's it."*

*You tell this chaplain your story. He is your only visitor. The only listener.*

I keep hearing this sort of story from my patients, the ones with no visitors: You had people, and you gave and gave and caved in to those people, compromised and denied yourself for those people. But those people who were called "community" left anyway, long after they had taken. There is a turning point, tipping point, a split in this story, when you recognized you didn't belong and probably never did.

You either stayed in silent dissonance,

or you left all the people you ever knew for their own sake.

Either way, it is diminishing. Either choice has a cost, has a grief of its own.

My patient tells me, "I got no one but me. I chose me. But it's lonely to just be me."

You might arrive at this dilemma:

You choose to stay in a community even when you must hide and compromise,

or you choose no longer to hide, but for that, you must leave them behind.

In other words: *Which loneliness is the better one?*

*To be lonely with others or lonely by yourself? Is it better to grieve the familiar alone, or grieve alone with the familiar?*

Is it better to be in a familiar crowd, but without an authentic voice?

Or is it better to be an authentic self, but without the familiar crowd?

The answer seems obvious: We'd like to choose ourselves, even if that means leaving the people we know. But if you're like me, your roots are tied up with them because they're all you've known. To leave is to unravel, to start over. It's not as simple as walking out a door. It seems easier to stay camouflaged. Remain close, in contradiction. Undercover. At a distance and dissonant. You might parrot the creed but internally abhor the dogma. Drifting in limbo is comfortable, where the fear of being found out is easier to manage than the unknown of being alone.

The ironic truth is this: We need *distance*, carefully created, for real community. By distance, I mean no longer blending in by chameleonlike compromise and conformity. But to be able to stand in a room as yourself. Just long enough with the door open that others would see you, as you. That requires the hard grief of boundaries and possible rejection. That probably means fewer people, not more. That probably means you'll have to consider walking away from the people you called friends, who were never really with you or for you, but around you, and they were only around for the parts you showed them.

I heard author and activist bell hooks say it like this: "We all long for loving community. It enhances life's joy. But many of us seek community solely to escape the fear of being alone. Knowing how to be solitary is central to the art of loving. When we can be alone, we can be with others without using them as a means of escape."[4]

For a while I paid the grief of losing myself so that I could have the approval of warm bodies nearby. I didn't want to pay the grief of losing anyone, so I divided myself into cross-sections of triple-faced code-switching, doling out percentages of a made-up persona to collect a Frankenstein quilt that I thought was a community but was only a stitched monster at the behest of my own comfort. *But I found this: The cost of losing myself is far higher than the cost of losing people who never knew me.* So I had to pick my grief. It was never an easy answer. But any time I picked someone else over me, I lost two people: them and myself.

Only with clear boundaries—appropriate distance between self and others—can we bear when we are unseen. Not an intentional aloofness. But rather, *congruency*: the degree to which our authentic selves are externally expressed. Even if that means pushing back those who presumably hold the keys.

It's the right type of *being alone* that has a chance, if at all, to get us through loneliness. The opposite of loneliness is not being with more people. It is courage. I wish I had a better word, something less obvious. But a thing like that, do you see it often? The courage for less, not more? The courage to be your own companion, to stomach living on your own for a while, alone?

This means, sometimes, that there are people who won't go with you. Not any further. They will not go with you in change. In crisis. With *you*. They're no longer safe. Or they never were. It means saying goodbye to someone who never was, because you showed them a version of you that never was either.

You may not have gotten to say goodbye. To the people who would not go with you.

I believe that, in some measure, you can still have the funeral. For those who would not go. Grieving those you had to leave.

*Can you picture the one who did not go with you?*
*What are the things you will miss about them?*
*What are the things you will not miss about them?*
*What cost did you pay for staying?*
*What has become new again in this loss?*

## OBJECTIVE LONELINESS: FINDING
## THE ONES ALONG THE WAY

*You are locked inside this body. You are dying.*

*Delta variant. The bad one, they said. Lungs nearly gone. Ventilator, sedated, gasping—but you can see, you can hear, through a fog, as your organs are failing.*

*You've hardly moved in a week. Or a month? What time is it? What is time?*

*Then in front of you sits a chaplain who is attempting a video call with your family.*

*The call is made. And you see your family. Your wife, your three children, your brother, your sister. They are smiling. Just barely.*

*"If you can hear us," they keep saying. "If you can see us."*

*It sounds like they are saying goodbye. They are saying goodbye.*

*This chaplain is holding the iPad. For a long time, it seems. His arms are shaking. He is looking away, attempting to offer some semblance of privacy. He probably could've made the call and left the iPad on a table. But he's here. At least someone is here.*

*Your wife has taken her phone to another room. She is asking, "Any sign, baby? Can you give me any sign?"*

*You want to sit up. Out of this bed. Off this machine. Off this floor where you've seen sheet after sheet pulled across. But this body. This vent. You are alone, but for this chaplain.*

*"Chaplain?" your wife asks. "Can you—would you pray now for him?"*

*He turns the iPad to himself. "Yes. I will pray."*

*Then he prays. And somehow, this chaplain, he sprinkles in every little bit and piece of everything your family has said in their goodbyes. He has been listening. He gets one detail wrong: You were married twenty-two years, not twenty-five. But he is painting your life in this prayer.*

*He finishes his prayer. And you see your own hand move up. Extended fingers, frayed ends of rebar. You smell the teeth in your mouth, feel your tongue across the endotracheal tube, taste a film of grime, and in your nostrils breathe through a hard pulp. You are in your body again. You move. You move your hand toward the screen. The chaplain's eyes widen.*

*Your family shouts. "You're moving! Moving! He's trying to say something!"*

*Around the vent, you try to say something. You touch the screen. You try.*

*The chaplain is looking hard. Please, chaplain.*

*The chaplain says, "I think he's saying, 'I miss you.'"*

*You look at the chaplain. You try to nod. Close enough.*

This is the sort of loneliness that I see more of: an unchosen, unwanted distance, people pulled away by a situation outside of their control. It was James who had outlived all his family, and told me,

*I'm not just lonely. I'm alone.*

It would be easy, easier, if loneliness was just about setting boundaries, picking the right people, remaining true. Then the solution might just be a doorway away.

But if my patients suffer from chronic illness, poverty, housing crisis, a severe mental illness, a physical disability, then the chances are that they have fewer and fewer people. When a patient's condition becomes "too much," their people often abandon them. These patients live inside bodies considered obsolete. Until their only remaining companion, their body, betrays them too. An unbearable condition is compounded by abandonment that leaves them feeling cursed.

I visit a patient whose only next-of-kin is her husband, but each time the patient's condition gets worse, the husband's connection gets more tenuous as he travels back in time to become a fiancé, then boy-friend, then friend, then neighbor—and then he's gone.

I ask a different patient about his network of support and he tells me that no one has visited. Yet his entire family is local. "They won't see me," he says, "because they say I always do this. They think I'm faking heart attacks. But the truth is, they don't want to deal with me dying."

Other patients are abandoned because they worked themselves out of every relationship they had. My patient tells me, "I don't know why my children won't talk to me. All I ever did was work hard for them." I want to point out what he is saying. Not that this is his fault. But that he has been deceived. He has been told his entry into community was by contributing his sweat instead of his tears.

Or it was social distancing, a necessity for a good reason, but still there is a cost. The chaplains and I ran iPads to patients with COVID, especially during the delta variant, making dozens of good-bye calls for our patients' families around the hour. Most of these patients were intubated and sedated. But I assumed they could hear, that they were here.

There is a spiritual philosophy that chaplains learn called the Intimate Stranger.[5] It's the idea that we can talk deeper with strangers because there is no history of judgment. No backlog of fights or disappointments or harsh words. Mental health professionals, for example, can sit at enough distance to be nonjudgmental, but sit close enough to empathize with every tear, every trauma, every twitch of the eye.

The hard part about loneliness is that we can become especially lonely with our closest loved ones. Two spouses in the same bed; teenage children with their parents; two childhood friends—sometimes the very expectation of the other person's affection creates a vacuum, a dull ache of longing. The other person might be tired or distracted, busy and full, or simply pulling away.

Familiar and anchored history is what gives weighted meaning, but it also makes clutter. The routine itself, the predictable rhythms of a long relationship, can become an autopilot—a comforting one, but we learn where to withdraw until it is a reflex. In familiarity, we dance around limitations and secrets and unspoken pains.

The promise of the Intimate Stranger is a liminal space that holds both depth and surprise at once. Close enough to tell all your secrets, far away enough not to be judged by them.

In Korea and Japan, you may have heard of the rent-a-stranger, whose job is to be a presence paid for their time.[6] Whether it is to be there for signing divorce papers, walking for graduation, or just a dinner for two, the stranger moves when you do, listens with intent, does not disrupt. Is this too much of a Stepford wife situation? Renting a robotlike companion who fits our idealistic whims? Just a warm body who won't challenge or question us? Or is it a deeper need for all of us, who wish for a presence that will not judge or jump to our rescue, but only join us in the moment as a warm and welcoming witness to our lives?

In Korea, there is a phenomenon called godoksa, an "unconnected death," also known as a "lonely death." Someone takes their own life, often a man, and is discovered days later. The number of godoksa has increased every year, from the elderly to the young.[7] There are many things to blame: exhausting work ethic, the near enslavement of corporations, the difficulty of maintaining family ties in a hardened world. But there is one thing I do not blame. I do not fault the person who has died. If they failed to find their people, did *they* fail? Is loneliness *your* fault? I cannot help but think that all the ways we are taught to succeed alone have also led us to die alone, a deathbed already a tomb.

The Intimate Stranger is not a strange new idea. From gym to swim class to dojos to therapy and yoga and AA, from rent-a-strangers to airport conversations to a chaplain performing last rites, we have always met in liminal spaces for halfway connections that make us whole.

Family and friends are, in the end, limited. Caregiver fatigue sets in. We are busy, dragged along in the gears of hustle and institution. And time keeps ticking, age keeps taking, we keep losing as we live. I advocate for these *mid-road connections*. We need these Intimate Strangers as advocates of dignity, especially for the "obsolete," for my patients, the ones with no next-of-kin or who are unheard in a packed room.[8] In the words of philosopher Martin Buber, "All real living is meeting."[9] If that means a ten-second conversation in a line at the grocery store, or the snippets of storytelling between nurse and patient, or a chaplain who sits at bedside for an hour, these are *visibility-making moments*.

Chaplains, mental health providers, nurses and physicians and social workers, educators and mentors—we all enter this liminal space. We dance between listening and providing a different perspective. We often listen with no footnotes or reference, which also means we have little bias, no overshadow of moralizing with "I told you so." We ease loneliness as embodied reminders that even if you are alone, it is not merely you alone, but *we* alone.

I have walked this secret and sacred alleyway space, where a lonely patient who has been abandoned can see one friendly face. We are open books to one another, and because we have no reference to old chapters, we freely write the new ones. Maybe my patient used up all his goodwill and third chances. Or maybe my patient had a loving family and they silently went out the back door because they could no longer handle every oozing orifice. Whatever the reason was before I walk in that door, I enter as a witness. I am a mid-road companion. If my patient is carrying the weight of their cross up a hill, then for a brief moment I am one of the bystanders who steps in to share the weight of that cross.

The closest of our family and friends cannot give everything they have all the time. For the loneliest of us, it can be too painful to invest in long-term friendships in our twilight years or in the hardest of our grief and abandonment.

But it is still possible to invest in these smaller connections. These mid-road companions.

I hope no one will dissuade you from this:

You can find real encounters, in pockets and corners, with strangers and unknown neighbors, in minutes at a time, and even if it is just this once, to break bread and share in this space is never a small thing.

On night shift at three in the morning, I get calls from four nurses.

"My patient just wants to talk to someone."

"Can you come by? She's had no visitors."

"I know it's late. Do you have a minute for them?"

"They're up. They won't stop crying. They're not religious. Just need anyone."

In the stillness of night, I am a witness to regrets, to confessions. Patients in crisis, or before surgery, or at deathbeds, they tell me things they have never shared, that they would never have shared. I am in the liminal, the in-between. Not family. Not a friend. Barely a stranger. But to witness even briefly? I catch death, but I catch life too. At the terminal, at the end, ready for the flight where all the world must travel, I sit with you before boarding, to see you off. We will never meet again. This is my advantage. And yours. Here, the loneliness lifts as a wind through the mist.

This is not a shortcut to depth. But neither is this selling it short. I have had visits that within minutes, we shared a lifetime. It may surprise you. It did me. But if you can imagine, having held your stories and tears and secrets so close for so long, then given permission to speak with no fear of judgment: The dam breaks. We look over the waterfall. My patient, in some way, always asks me, "Is this okay?"

Yes, I tell them. You are okay. Yes. Fall freely. Break freely. This is where you can give your dam.

Our loneliness is a perpetual question of our own significance. Who will touch the monuments you have carved from these castles of sand? Who will see your work like so much graphite that dissipates with every turn of the page? Who will know you as you know yourself, and still hold?

For a lifetime or this time or the last time, can we exchange life and trust, that up this quiet road, we may walk each other home?

## A COMMUNION OF BREAKING BREATH WITH STRANGERS

*You are in a private waiting room. The Emergency Department.*

*You've just been told your father has died. The physician tells you they tried everything. You hardly hear it. You find yourself alone, with the chaplain.*

*He tells you, almost in a whisper, that he's sorry. He says he can escort you to the back to see your father. He offers to answer any questions about the next step in the process. And then he says this peculiar thing.*

*"I just wanted you to know—I know this might not be very helpful— but I was there the whole time. We were there. He was never alone the entire time."*

*You never imagined your dad dying this way. Surrounded by the flurry of a medical team, not with a single one of his family around him.*

*"I called for a moment of silence," this chaplain says, "and I said his name out loud. We had a moment to honor your dad."*

*Maybe this is your only relief. To know this chaplain was there. A team was there. He wasn't alone when he died. And for a second, they knew him. They saw him. A patient and a person.*

*"Chaplain, thank you for telling me this. I didn't know that I needed to know it."*

Sometimes no one. Nothing. No family. All I can do is hold my patient's hand. Watch his heart rate dwindle to single digits. Hear his last wishes. His last breaths. He does not know me. I do not know him. He holds my hand tightly to the end.

*No one can die alone. No one must die alone.*

The pager goes off. Code Blue. I hope it's canceled. I wait. Two minutes. Five. Not canceled. I excuse myself from my current patient visit. He has a GSW. Gunshot wound. Handcuffed to the bed and there is an officer watching us. My patient asks me to come back. Pleading eyes above a mask. I am his only visitor.

Dash down the hall. Patients flash by. Ventilators and BiPap and IV bags hanging like birthday balloons. Stories. They matter. I want to stop at each one. See them and hear them. Too many won't make it home. They'll be alone.

The Code Blue is a COVID patient. I hate calling them that. They're more. The rapid-response team dons their gear. Gloves, gown, goggles, N95. Negative pressure room. Touch nothing. But the patient. Compressions. It's probably the first time anyone has touched the patient all week. Chemicals: vaso, epi, bicarb. They will break his ribs. To raise a human life requires an unthinkable amount of exertion and pain. I calculated once how much it costs. At least a dozen people in the team, each person with years of education and experience, aided by equipment and medicine and research, every person involved from front door to sanitation to maintenance: about a thousand years per patient. It takes life for life.

One hour. No pulse. Does anyone have any ideas? Time of death. I call for a moment of silence. If I know the name of the patient, I name them. Report. Clean. Turn over the room. Chaplain, ready?

We call the family. He died. Will you be seeing your loved one?

The family cannot come. They all have COVID too. They're inconsolable. He was fine a week ago. No one could say goodbye. "Can I see him?" I offer a video call. I try to prepare them. They see him. It is hard. They see him.

The pager goes off. MVC. Pedi. Car accident, child. The pager goes off again. Car accident. Same one? Maybe mother or father. Pager goes off again. Running. I hear her. She is maybe five or six. Calling for Mom. Mom follows. Diffuse axonal injury. Dad follows. I see bone. When the whole family comes in from the same accident, what family do I call?

I see the dad. "I hear them. Can I see them?" The team swirls. We arrange for the dad to see his daughter. He sees her. It is hard. But he sees her.

It is what we need. I run to be eyes and ears.

The pager doesn't stop. I don't either.

I barely make it back to my first patient. The GSW.

"Chap, I'm glad you came back," he says. "No one usually does."

"I see you," I tell him. I see him through tears. "I am here."

I run from room to room, to every death. I try to catch death. I try to beat death.

I make it. I don't make it. We find family. Too late. Flight landed late. Sometimes it lands early. A patient breathes two more minutes, as if waiting. Waiting for family. Or for me, the only witness. *No one can die alone.* But they do. They do. I can't let it happen. It happens. I am running. Trying. I might be the last one you see. A stranger. But I can't let you die alone.

*At the end, who will I see? Loved ones, I hope. But anyone, rather than no one.*

I stay, as long as they need. This is it. It is flesh-and-bone presence that we need. One who does not leave. One who speaks life into death. One who ensures that those who have no one have someone.

We do not, in the end, always find next-of-kin. But maybe we can be "caught and welcomed by a tenderness in kinship."[10] If not the next-of-kin, then next-*to*-kin. I think of the arms-stretched Christ uttering these final words, his one and singular command: to his mother, *Behold, your son*, and to his beloved friend John, *Behold, your mother*.[11] Kinship, not a fix, but a balm. And I consider how the resurrected Jesus returned to his disciples, their futures muddled, each huddled behind locked doors, hiding from hunting, and I am moved by the shape of their joined shoulders. I imagine that even if Sunday had not come, even if the tomb had remained sealed, what these disciples found in the silence of a sealed room was a communion of breath, anxious yet abiding in one another. What they found in the gap between wood and stone were their hands reaching in tender and tangible vicinity.

When I consider what it is to have faith, to clutch the edge of hope in the middle of our suffering, this is how I believe we experience God entering, how I hope to enter too: with hands, feet, eyes, and the heart of the divine in a room at the corner of the universe. Saint John said it like this: "No one has ever seen God, but if we love one another, God lives in us and his love is made complete in us."[12] If we are made for each other, then our separation is a wound, and when we meet, it is grace that enters there and mends us together.

I am a witness, momentarily. My patient's loneliness is seen. It does not fix it. It cannot. No one's loneliness *can* be fixed. But there is something valuable, holy, sacred about being seen. I have held hands with patients who did not want to die alone—and it did not entirely matter then that I was a stranger. It mattered that someone was there. Each of us *will* die alone, behind the opaque walls of our own minds. Yet there is value in being lonely hand in hand.

For long seasons, you may be lonely. I can only tell you, your hand in mine:

*We are*

*(not)*

*alone.*

# eight

# LOSS OF LOVED ONES: YOU GO, I GO

## The problem with "moving on," and how we "move with" instead

Content warning: This chapter contains descriptions of traumatic loss, including loss in resuscitation, and infant loss. Reader, please be advised.

*Chia buồn: a Vietnamese phrase that means "to divide sadness," and is used to express condolences. It implies the communal sharing of grief together.*

## WHEN IT HAPPENS: GRIEF IS DEFIANCE

The second I see my friend John at the hospital, I know he's gone. I have seen this too many times, heartbeats extracted only by machine.

I had gotten the call from my supervisor, who said John had been in an accident.

I have known John for a year. A work friend. But we have become close outside of work. And John has ended up on my assigned floor.

Room 5116K. I'll never forget the room number. For five days I visit John at the hospital, be with his family, then back to the hospital floor. I'm holding grief while grieving. Back and forth. Restroom break to weep. Back to John's room. And on the fifth day, his family decides to let him be at peace.

I'm with my fellow chaplain as I say goodbye. Laura. She puts a hand on my shoulder as I weep over John's body.

Pockets of memories come through. I remember how John randomly sent me these exclamatory text messages. "Put on shades and be a light in the darkness!" Or, "Don't sell yourself short!" Or, "The world is your gym!" He took the last one seriously. He sent me a video of himself outside his house lifting bricks for weights. It took a long explanation to understand what I was looking at. I remember John always showing me pictures of his almost-one-year-old, endless rows of pictures, and how he could talk for forty minutes straight without inhaling, all the while smiling.

John had this lizard at his desk who came to visit once in a while, but one day John found the lizard had died in his drawer so we held a funeral for it. A brave explorer, John had called it. He used a paper clip for the cross at its headstone, which he made of a tinfoil wrapper from a chocolate bar. It was morbid and absurd and somber, and I tried not to break during the eulogy. But everything about this was very much John.

I lean over to him, to say something. The only sound is his machine breathing.

There are a lot of recorded last words by those who are dying. But most of the time, no one knows when they'll get to say their last words. Usually, it's the other way around. It's the living who say their last words to the dying.

I can't think of anything.

I remember how the nurses and physicians always say, "Hearing is the last thing to go," and I want to say something to send him off, to be at ease.

"John."

I clutch the edge of his bed. Something like anger rips through me.

"We were supposed to get Korean barbecue. We were supposed to—"

He sent me a text the day before his accident. "Just a lot going on." It had me worried. His last text to me, on the day of the accident: "Hopefully see ya tomorrow." Only two hours later, his accident happened. I should've dropped everything. Gone to him. I had just gone on. Back to everything else. I'm angry at myself. Can't forgive myself. But it was an accident. An accident. He slipped. But what if I had just—

"I should have—"

I can only think of how unfair this is. Why him.

I let out a long breath. I wish I had more.

I used to think that grief was about acceptance.

But—to accept the loss of the one you love is too much like approving death. A betrayal of their life.

I need to tell you about one patient who left me with no doubt that all my ideas about grief, loss, death—had been wrong.

My patient is a teen. Time of death is called. But his father continues compressions.

His father is a physician. The team watches. Unsure. Our patient's grandfather is walking circles around the room. Clapping, praying, laughing, weeping, shouting over and over, "I trust you. This is not right but I trust you."

The attending steps in. Says, quietly, "I'm sorry, Roy. He's gone. Your son is gone."

"No," Roy says. He slaps away hands. "No. You know I can't stop."

The stitches pop open. Roy's son. Heart transplant. It had worked for a week. Then crashed, fast.

"Baby boy," Roy says to his son. Compressions. "Baby boy. You can't go like this. Don't leave like this."

The attending speaks again. Harder this time. "Roy, I am sorry. But he is gone."

"No!" Roy's tears and sweat mix. His father is still pacing. Praying out loud.

"Roy."

"You know I can't stop. You know that."

"You have to."

"You know I can't. *You know I cannot stop.*"

"Roy. Roy. Listen, Roy. *Dr. Simmons.* Please."

Roy turns away from the attending and towards me. He grabs my shoulders hard. Says to me, "He wasn't supposed to go. Tell everybody I can't stop. Would *you* stop? Come on, would you?"

"No," I tell him. "I wouldn't."

"Do this for me," he says. "I did what I could. I need you to pray for him. God can bring him back. I know it. I know God can do it."

Roy's father joins us. Clapping, shouting, "Yes. Yes, he can."

They are on both sides of me. I am standing over my patient, Matthew.

"Dr. Simmons, I'm not—"

*I'm not sure this is the right thing to do.*

I've seen churches do this. Revive the dead. For a low, low price. Exploit faith. Spectacle. She's not dead. Just believe. Just pray. Just pay. But. I think this is not that.

Roy grabs my hands. Mouths the words, *Please pray.* Again: *Please pray.*

"Okay," I tell him. "Okay. I'll pray."

I place both my hands on Matthew. On his open stitches. I'm still not sure this is okay. I pray. I am praying for God to revive my patient.

I have prayed this before. Standing to the side, watching a Code Blue, twenty, thirty, forty minutes, pulse check, epi, bicarb, resume compressions. I have prayed for a resurrection. *I'm only asking for a miracle, God. A single sneeze in our direction. This one time, surprise us. Make me believe in something again. He wasn't supposed to go.*

My palms rest on a reopened incision. It's still warm. I know he is dead. His father and grandfather are praying loudly. I know he is dead. I pray. What else can I do? I know he is dead. Because, because—

*Death is a switchblade that will not retract.*

*The blade takes. What spills will not be refilled.*

I am in this room for a long time. The prayers go silent. The team left a while ago. First, Roy removes his hands. Then his father. They know he is dead.

Roy leans over to his son. He tells him, "Son. You go, I go."

*You go, I go.*

Roy falls to the floor. Takes me down with him. His father slumps in a chair at bedside. We three hold this way. In defiance of death, we weep.

I have seen, too many times, when resuscitations go too far.

But I can understand it. How can anybody stand it, to extinguish even the smallest flicker of life?

I got into the work of grief expecting a lot of solemn, somber

moments at the bedsides of dying people. Last words, lights soften-
ing, peaceful ships crossing over, once in a while even the screaming.
What I was not prepared for was the sheer depth of anxiety and rage
at death. The terror of it, but also the audacity. An unthinkable insult,
a mocking cruelty. *How dare this life be taken. How dare you die on
me. How dare you leave me like this. Wake up. Get up. You hear me. You
have to get up.*

A bereaved spouse asks me, "Why? Why even do this? Is it worth
it? Worth loving somebody to see them go?"

I want to say yes. And no. I don't know. I'd like to think so. Is it?
When you know what's coming?

The death of a person, its intractability, *Never Here Again,* to see the
one you love go under the impermeable, is an incomprehensible absurdity. To accept the fact of *Never Here Again* is, on its face, insulting.

Death is a permanent curtain of the ocean thrown over a life. We
the living try to pull back at the edge of water to reach under. But an
ocean cannot be subdued. Never unraveled. There is no stitch at the
horizon. The skyline is airtight.

Who can accept a thing like that?

What I had once believed about loss was that it followed the lin-
ear nature of time, not perfectly and not easily, but at the very least a
stumbling forward until loss was absorbed into the unclenched hands
of acceptance. And I had thought I was more gracious than most. *It's
your tempo, your pace, there are no stages or phases, have grace for yourself.*

But I have to admit this to you. I was less gracious than I really
knew. Much less.

Nobody, not a single person I've met, could accept a thing like
death with ease. And why should they? Why should I? Why should you?

I want to tell you that *you don't have to.* Not the way you've been
told you should.

First, I need to tell you what happened to me. Something strange happened after seeing so much death, something that changed my vision, something that's still happening now.

You'd think after a while that I would get used to all the dying. Body after body, countless deathbeds, that maybe I'd just find it routine. But that much death did something else to me. The shape of every loss slithered its way into my veins. It changed my vision. It altered something deep, irrevocably.

Here's when I knew. A couple years in, I'd look someone in the eye in a casual conversation, and then it was as if lightning struck behind them. I'd see their skeleton. Or pale flesh on a slab. Or a laceration, their neck in a C-collar, their chest getting compressed, a zipper over their head. I'd have the thought, *What if this is it? The last time I talk to this person? The last laugh we share? The last meal?* Always could be the last. On their way home. Randomly. I'd seen it hundreds of times, a casual day turned into a Level 1 trauma with your clothes cut in half by a paramedic and floating faces in masks keeping your blood intact. I couldn't stop seeing it. The living dead. The Last Time.

Maybe this whole Last Time thing sounds like a blessing in disguise. Makes you appreciate life or something like that. Maybe. But it's not easy holding the dead. The vicarious grief I accumulated at bedside gave me an anticipatory grief: Everyone around me became as transparent as sand in the wind. Eventually, I couldn't look at somebody across from me without wanting to grab their face and freeze time. I'd picture gripping a corner of their soul, pulling and looping around my hand, an entire strand digging into the crease of my palm, and tying it around my wrist, my elbows, my waist, keeping them here, safe. I had the absurd notion of climbing people like they were trees and then sitting on their heads, refusing to get down, as if the tree of their life couldn't be cut down if I refused to leave.

Memories were shards. They cut me in dreams. Anytime I'd depart some place, I'd bleed something, losing time, we had so little, each moment spent apart was another one cast backward into the fire. I got obsessed with checking clocks, counting seconds, counting breaths, words, heartbeats, bites of food. I couldn't sleep because my dreams were about my patients, closing in, and I was convinced my sleep was more lost time that I could be alive, with the living, for the last time.

What I was experiencing was a sort of *death anxiety*. And it was telling me something true.

Every time I was anxious about someone in front of me dying, I had tried to etch that moment into marble. Capture the time, a diorama in a snow globe, this memory a rerun on repeat. My anxiety, as far as I knew, was not unreasonable. Only revealing.

I was experiencing a truth about grief that demolished what I used to believe.

*Grief is not acceptance of death. Grief is a defiance of death.* What I mean is, grieving is not burying someone to keep them behind you. That's suppression. That's forgetting. Grieving is bringing them forward instead, the dead defiantly brought back to life.

My death anxiety was saying this to the living: *Tomorrow I will lose you. So I am here with you today, that you will be here with me tomorrow, and tomorrow still.*

*In this defiant grief, loss is pulled closer. Your loss is not cast behind you but made alive before you now.*

There is an ironic inversion that occurs when you suppress grief.[1] The more you attempt to bury the dead, the more likely they will burst through your everyday. You awaken again to the nightmare that they are gone. But—bringing them alive, moments at a time, is a way of holding their loss close.

Your body knows it already. Your body defies attempts to move on. Your body bursts with the story of their life. This needs pause. It needs voice.

I do not, not for a moment, ease my patients or their families into acceptance of death. But instead, when a patient dies, for as long as the family needs, we bring them back to life.

Here is what I mean. For every patient who is dying or has died, I ask their family:

*What was she like?*

*What was he like?*

*What sort of person were they?*

It is a painful question. Not everyone answers. But for some, grieving this way, with the briefest resurrection, is what they need most right then.

To tell the story, to lift the lost up one more time, to encapsulate a lifetime in sentences—often the words rush out, like they had been waiting to tell the story.

Grief emerges defiantly, a life story bursting forth from the tomb.

I visit a patient, Rhonda. Her family surrounds her. Her time of death was only minutes ago. Her husband, Jimmy, is holding her hand.

We sit in silence for a while. The stillness is palpable. Single movements, a curtain shifting, a chair squeaking, it is all too loud. My father used to say that even one piece of dust is heavy on the dead. Death creates such a vacuum that the world pulls away and presses in at the same time.

I ask Jimmy, "What was Rhonda like?"

For a second, just one, he laughs. Without pausing, Jimmy tells me, "Rhonda was a sweet, sweet lady. We loved to get away. We had this hatchback, we'd pack up enough to last us a couple days, and we'd stretch that out for a week. When it's you and the road, a can of Spam can last as long as you want it to. I had this broke-down fishing rod, but my wife had all the luck with that. There was this one place, it's exactly how you'd picture it: a thick wall of trees and suddenly there's a lake inside, like turning the page of a coloring book and someone's painted it before you got there. I'd set up the fishing rod and my wife was the Pied Piper. All the fish just danced to her. We'd grill the fish right there in front of a blue crystal ocean. We'd sit shoulder to shoulder over the fire and eat the fish with our hands. It was so messy. It was so funny, to eat that way. Our laughing carried over the water. Does that sound like a fairy tale? It was, my man. It was. We traveled like that to the end."

One by one, her family tells me about her.

Each person has a different story, angle, facet, texture, the edges of a person's life. At one point someone recounts a funny thing Rhonda used to do. And they laugh. Until they slap their knees, push shoulders, laugh until tears stream down. I think of laughter over water, over the lake.

I can almost see her. I weep for this family, who must move into a world that will move without her.

I am reminded of the Korean concept of 정 (Jeong), the warmth of a close bond, that which compels us to see and care for one another, in the ways we offer our food and our tears, in how there is no Korean phrase for "my home," but it is 우리 집 (oori-jib), *our* home. I believe that to remember our dead, even briefly, is to experience Jeong with our departed, to return to the warmth of our home, built of memory.

From such Jeong can emerge 흥 (Heung), an ecstatic joy, a soaring exhilaration.[2] In so many rooms, I have often felt Jeong and even Heung, between me and the patient and family and providers, and in this rift of loss, we huddle closer, close enough to carry one another, just as water carrying the sound of laughter. I recall the words of the prophet Zephaniah, about the God who delights in us, sings over us rejoicing[3]—and I imagine between the echoes of grief in this carved valley of loss, we find wellsprings of delight in one another as God does, sheer and unalloyed joy, not only a remedy, but the reason we are here.

I am a catcher of grief and of bodies—once in a while I get the honor of catching joy too.

As the family leaves, the husband leans over his wife. He whispers to her, "I'll see you again, my love." He sweeps her hair. Touches her hand. Looks into her face. "I will see you at our lake. Our parting is only a short while."

## THE SPACE AFTERWARD: GRIEF IS EVERYTHING AND ANYTHING ALL AT ONCE

*liget: a word used by the Ilongot to describe "high voltage" emotion, emerging as animated rage for either destruction or creation*[4]

I used to think that grief had a singular, common expression, a somber response of tears and sadness.

I used to think that grief needed time, needed activity and direction.

What I did not expect is that grief can look like everything. It can need anything.

We grieve differently, as much as we need differently.

Two phone calls. I tell both of them, "Your husband is at the hospital."

One screams, drops the phone, picks it back up, asks a dozen questions, stays on while driving. The other is silent, shocked, no noise but the road.

Both, I believe, are valid responses. Our bodies cling to what we need to survive the moment, even the smallest plank in the hardest sea.

Death steals more than the room. It steals composure.

One of the most realistic depictions of grief I've seen in a movie is from *The Host*, directed by Oscar-winning filmmaker Bong Joon-Ho. In the movie, a monster has apparently killed dozens of people. There is a vigil at a gymnasium with shrines of the victims' pictures. We follow a family that mourns at the picture of a young girl. She was the youngest member of their family. The scene is bewildering. The family screams the young girl's name, falls over backward, the young girl's uncle slaps his brother in the head and throws a jump kick at him, they wrestle on the ground, photographers surround them and snap photos, and a first responder enters loudly declaring that someone needs to re-park their car outside. It is frantic, unflinching, even funny. Any film critic would tell you there is no *tonal consistency*.

No tonal consistency.

I have never seen tonal consistency in grief.

My ideas about dying were half-formed by Hollywood, sculpted by serene and romantic imagery. In reality, grief rarely looks like that. I've seen the living throw their bodies across the dead, wracked by convulsions, heaves and sobs, limbs and chair legs and purses turned over, sweat and stink. I've seen bodies in grief as still as sheets. I've seen so many scratch their own faces in horror, or eyes glued to phones scrolling in digital dreamscapes, to distract and detach, to avoid looking into the floor of the sea where death is unreturned.

I have been in rooms where the family is wailing, blubbering, dancing, pacing, rocking, rolling on the floor, punching themselves, narrating their emotions, singing, cussing, laughing, vomiting, screaming.

I have been in rooms where there is numbness, no tears, blank faces, hiding, falling asleep, flat affect, whispering, hardly able to speak a sentence, even a guilty sense of boredom when the death is long and lingering.

There are both *extreme expressions of emotion* and *complete deflation of the body*.

Some may say it's too much. Or fake. Or laughable.

Some say grief has to be:

not too much and not too little,

just enough tears to see you care,

but too many then you have to leave,

controlled, calm, measured, even-toned, but if you're numb then what's wrong with you,

no smiling or laughing or else you don't mean it,

completely somber, no heaving and shouting and no weird noises.

I have wondered if false beauty standards have shaped how we see grieving: as a metric meant to grade our own morality of sadness, rather than a real visceral reaction that needs to be voiced.

From all my years in the hospital, I have seen this: There is no polished, solemn version of grief on a single charted path. It will be piercing, jarring, never Hollywood. It is filled with noises and movements you did not know a body could make. It will be extreme, or internalized; it is loud, or hardly a sound. In some rooms, the grief is an almost embarrassing release. Not everyone has to weep, not right then. Some need to laugh. Or eat. Or organize. Or sleep.

All of it, anything and everything, is grief. And it is true.

I know this. Grief cannot be evaluated or qualified. Everyone grieves the way they will.

And just as each of us grieves differently, each of us needs something different to get us through.

*Mono no aware: a Japanese idiom meaning "the awareness of transience." It is the gentle sadness over the impermanence of all things. It is the sense that in the reality of our inevitable passing, we can find beauty and meaning in the fleeting.*

Every loss leaves a love-shaped gash that was formed around the one you loved.

To lose the one you love is more than losing half of you, but at once, it is a sudden evulsion of a thread from your body and your memory, ripping away at numerous fixtures, leaving a crevice.

That crevice, the shape of that loss, never looks the same for anyone.

Grief is a universal feeling, an ancient language. But two people who speak the same language will still speak with their own speed and timbre, their rise and fall, their volume and velocity.

I do not assume that your comfort or mine, your need or mine, are ever the same. My fellow chaplain Larry once told me, "Grief takes up a lot of space." It takes what it needs to. The things that patients tell me:

"I'm sorry for crying."

"I'm sorry for rambling."

"I'm sorry to put that on you."

"I'm sorry—"

I assure them, in word and posture and presence, they are never too much.

You are never too much. Vent, cuss, weep, shout, ramble, repeat. I'm here.

When families throw chairs, I let them be. They must. I understand safety. I know when it is safer to leave. It is simply this: Chairs can be replaced. But hearts? Give them all the chairs.

I am called to a dying patient. The family has asked for information about funeral arrangements. I arrive to a big family. They share stories about their loved one. He was so carefree, to the point of being forgetful. Once he forgot about hosting a family dinner so he threw a bunch of frozen meals on the grill. They share story after story like this. Suddenly, the family is smiling, almost giggling. But they seem almost afraid to laugh, as if it is wrong.

One of the family members then asks about the funeral information. I check my clipboard and I realize I haven't brought it.

I tell them, "So, um . . . I forgot to bring it."

And this family roars with laughter. They double over crying, slapping their legs, unable to hold it anymore. One of them asks for a tissue because they're crying so hard. I promptly hold up a new box of tissues from my jacket. This erupts a new wave of laughing. Even guffawing, if you can believe it. There is much needed relief, the needed *Heung*.

Anyone looking in might have thought, *How could they laugh right now?*

And I can only think, *How can we not?* How can we hold back the holiness of being fully human, in all our loss and love?

"Are you the hamburger guy?"

Word has gotten around. I've become the hamburger chaplain.

"That's you, right? I know it's you. You got, like, generous-type eyes."

His wife, my patient, is CMO, Comfort Measures Only. She is breathing her last. Her husband at bedside is asking me for a hamburger.

"Can I get two?" he asks me.

I get him two hamburgers. With two large fries. He weeps and eats his hamburgers. Eats and weeps. He finishes the last of his fries as his wife dies.

I guess, through a window, it doesn't look right. Who eats when their wife is dying?

But then, who hasn't wanted to eat during the worst of their grief?

Who has been afraid to ask for the thing they needed in their grieving because they didn't want to be judged for it?

The husband licks his fingers as I go over the release form.

"I'm sorry," he tells me. "I'm sorry for eating like this. I just. I'm just. It's just. You know?"

"I know."

"Thank you for the fries too."

I think about that widower who needed a hamburger while his wife left her body.

I think about the family who had taken videos of their matriarch, *Our mother.*

I think about Raneeta, who needed me to reassure her that she had made the right decision, asking me, *What would you have done?*

I think about Marika, who needed a picture of her son Charles, and how I sat down with Marika in the hallway for two hours, and I did not say a word.

Have you been afraid to ask for the thing you needed in your grieving because you didn't want to be judged for it?

Always I am asking this question, out loud or by reading the room: *What do you need right now?*

It's a hamburger and fries, or photos and videos, or wisdom about a decision, or to sit in a hallway together.

What we need for grief is anything and everything that fits us right now.

Sometimes you won't know exactly what you need until someone helps meet that need.

I recognize that what I pass along as a chaplain gets passed along. In other words, the way I hold somebody's grief might show them a way to hold somebody's grief.

Here's what I mean. I meet a family in the waiting room to escort them to see their loved one in the trauma bay. On this shift, a busy one, I can only take one family member at a time. I always prepare family who's going back, to soften the shock. I'll say something like, "I'm going to bring you back through the trauma bay. You might see a lot of hospital activity. Your loved one is also still attached to a lot of equipment, and I want to prepare you that they won't look the way you last saw them."

When I bring the first family member back to the waiting room, she says to the next family member almost the same words I've said: "We're going back to the trauma bay, and there's a lot of stuff back there. She's attached to a lot of equipment. She won't look like she did yesterday." To prepare them. And down the line it goes. The softness is passed along. Each giving the next one what they didn't know they needed.

I've learned: *The way you are held in the aftermath of grief very often becomes how you hold yourself and others the rest of the way.*

In the seconds, hours, weeks after loss—what fills this space is crucial.

What fills the sudden void of loss can become the path on which the bereaved will walk for a lifetime. There are no perfect words, but there are harmful mouths, and there are words that help no one.

What I have tried to offer in words is this:

*You're going to get a lot of unhelpful words, and there really are no words for what you're going through.*

A guy in his twenties comes in, Arik. He's been in a car accident that killed three of his friends. Arik was the designated driver.

The second I enter the room, he asks, "Can I see them?" Before I can answer, he howls, "I killed them, I killed them, I killed my best friends. *It should've been me.*" He balls up his fists and hits his own forehead, yelling his friends' names in long, anguished cries.

A long time passes. He turns to me, as if he's just seen me. His eyes are wide, and he waits for me to say something. I realize this is one of those rare moments: He really needs me to offer something.

"Arik." I speak slowly, almost a whisper. "I'm sorry. I wish I had some magic formula or the right series of words to make it better. But the truth is—-this is going to be terrible for a long, long time. You'll feel it the rest of your life. It will hit you in waves. You'll be walking down the street or turning a corner in your house, and something will remind you of your friends. People will ask you a lot of questions. Some people might believe you, and others are going to hate you. You might hate yourself sometimes. Everyone will tell you how to be and how you shouldn't be, they'll tell you to 'cheer up' and 'get over it' or 'it'll be all right.' Eventually, you might learn to live inside your own head, but it'll always be a fight. I'm telling you all this so you won't be too surprised. I'm trying to be honest with you, because maybe a lot of people won't be."

Arik reaches up to clasp my hand. He grabs it, hard.

# LIVING AFTER DYING: GRIEF IS GOING WITH

*"Some say rich people are those who have rich memories."*

— KIM SAE-BYUL, A TRAUMA CLEANER SPECIALIZING IN 특수청소 (TEUK-SO CHANG-SUH), THE CLEANING OF BELONGINGS OF THOSE WHO HAVE DIED ALONE.[5]

I used to think grief was about letting go and moving on. I no longer think that is true.

Grief is not letting go. It is letting in. Grief is not moving on. It is moving with.

"What you told me yesterday," my patient says, out of breath, "kept me up all night."

A day ago, my patient Ramses told me he and his daughter had been in a house fire. They were both hospitalized. After two weeks, Ramses made it. His daughter was intubated, then crashed, and she never recovered. Ramses watched his daughter die just four beds away from his own.

"What you told me," he says again, "got me doing okay right now."

Ramses says every person in his life was telling him the same thing:

"Let go. It's time to move on from this. You got to move forward. A couple years is long enough."

He weeps through this, telling me, "I tried to grieve this but I must be doing it all wrong."

At that, I am angry for him. I can only tell him, "How can anyone really move on from that sort of loss? What if you don't have to move on from her, but you can move *with* her? Keep her with you? What if moving forward means letting her life fill up your life?"

I worry it was too much. Ramses nods a bit, shares a little more, then tells me, "I have to think about that one." I am sure I've lost him.

He calls for me the next day. And says, "Trying to get over my daughter just made everything harder. I was putting all this work into pushing her away. I'd think about her and then take twice as much time trying not to think about her. After you said what you said, you know what it was like for me? It was like, carrying my daughter made me lighter. Like I got the strength. From her. I'm taking her with me, chap. She's going with me."

One of the chaplains, Amy, leads us through an exercise to release our grief. The secondhand, residual, vicarious, accumulated grief. From everything we see, everything we hold.

We commemorate a patient by telling their story out loud. Then place a colored glass stone in a glass jar. It sounds simple. But it is more visceral than I had thought it would be.

I find it impossible to let go of the stones. Every *clink* around the room plucks a nerve inside me. It seems unfair. I want to keep the memories of my patients, as if I owe them, as if I am somehow tarnishing their lives by dropping them.

I think of each of my patients' names that week. There are too many. I say them slowly, tell their stories in a whisper. Earlier that day, I remember four trauma alerts, every name important, a wound in their side a wound in mine. I unfurl my fist. *Clink.* I remember an exchange, a back-and-forth, some realization my patient had. *Clink.* Tears they wept, laughter they shared. *Clink.* Prayers prayed. *Clink.* And I look in this glass jar. Here they are. Glass stones in a glass. And I think, maybe, placing them here is okay. I want to keep these memories, and I'm keeping them. This is the ritual, to honor them, not by letting go, but by lifting up. I'm reminded of this quote by Carrie Fisher: "Because, after all, nothing is ever really over. Just over there."[6]

I trust that I have honored them, treasures in glass jars.

Ritualizing, as far as it can, honors the unresolved.

Ritualizing. To remember the dead. Routinely mark the moment. Highlight who they were. This reconciles, not completely, but continually, the significance of their loss and life.

There is a story told by professor Mary-Frances O'Connor of a widow, Vivian, who continues to cook two meals each night, but she always throws one away. Her grief is compounded: Her husband had been in the hospital awhile, but the moment Vivian had returned home to rest, he had died. The meals were a way to continue feeding her husband, to assuage her guilt, to deal with her loneliness.

She takes on CGT, Complicated Grief Treatment. I had assumed here that the therapist, like many in traditional therapy, would attempt to get to the root of her "dysfunction," to get her to stop cooking the extra meal. But he doesn't. Instead, the therapist asks her to find a way to use the unfinished food. Vivian finds out that her church serves homebound parishioners who would love a home-cooked meal. Vivian is eventually able to give her second meal over to the church to feed those who cannot leave their homes.[7]

A woman named Nikhita Kini had her late father's shirts turned into quilts. She says, "It was a ritual for mom and me to pick his shirts for him according to the colour of his pants. He would literally call us if we were away to ask us the correct combinations.[8] A man in Singapore who lost his grandmother to cancer continues to find her picture on Google Maps. He says he visits her to tell her he is doing okay.[9] Joan Didion shares how she gave away all of her late husband's clothing, but she decided to keep his shoes, writing, "I stood there for a moment, then realized why: he would need shoes if he was to return."[10]

In the hospital, we use embossing powder to create a handprint of a dying patient. We call this *memory-making* or *legacy-making*. One of my fellow chaplains, Tommy, processes the grief of his work by writing haikus about his patients. In Korean families, we commemorate death-days of our ancestors in a ceremony called 제사 (jesa). The deceased mother or father is celebrated, stories shared, a meal prepared.

This is more than moving on. This is moving *with* loss, their life enlarging yours, moving with their memory preserved in glass. I know you'd rather they be here. But grieving, in the way that you need, is embraced as it is. Not to be denied, but held. The room is expanded. It includes the pain and its story. The story is continued.

## A WHOLE AND REAL LOSS

*Brief were my days among you,*
*and briefer still the words I have spoken.*
*But should my voice fade in your ears, and*
*my love vanish in your memory,*
*then I will come again,*
*And with a richer heart and lips more yielding to the spirit will I speak.*
— KAHLIL GIBRAN, "THE FAREWELL"[11]

Over Easter weekend, my wife has a miscarriage. She is bleeding on Good Friday, and we go to the hospital on Saturday, my hospital, while I am on shift. I am given permission to see her between patient visits. My wife, now my patient. My unborn daughter, now my patient. Between grief, I am grieving. We are told the loss is due in part to it being a *pregnancy of unknown location*. I learn words like *manual vacuum aspiration, methotrexate, HCG, ectopic*. I can't stop repeating: *unknown location*.

We can't stop weeping. Why would we? It is a real loss. We lost a whole person. *A dream of unknown location. Name, plans, hopes: unknown location*. Not a shape, not a sketch, but a whole and real person. I had dreamed of her. She is gone. She lives in the home of another world.

I have heard bad advice, some at past bedsides, and some for us that weekend. The implication that it was my wife's fault. Or the pacification that, "You can make another one." Or, "At least you already have one." Or, "At least it wasn't a real baby." I remember this is not always malicious. Loss sends us looking for words, hands slip at their edges, we are rendered anxious at the unknown.

We tell our two-year-old daughter. She is silent for an hour. It's unlike her. Then she asks several times, "How come baby gone?" I don't know what to say. I am asking the same thing. I keep asking.

On Sunday I am dropped off at the hospital to pick up my car. I had to leave it the day before to drive my wife home; she'd had an invasive procedure and was not allowed to drive. I catch the Easter service at the hospital chapel. I am unmoved by the story of the resurrection. Who gets to live? Who has to die? Who makes it? Why? I see too many futures cut short. Cut fast. We are paper lanterns and the fire is sudden. The briefest flicker and then, vapor. I don't see many Sundays. Mostly I see Fridays. Mostly I live in the loss of Saturday.

At the end of the service, a fellow chaplain asks if I could close the service with a prayer. I haven't been part of the planned proceedings. She doesn't know what I am holding. I could easily refuse. But I walk to the podium in front of my coworkers—each of us intimate with death— and my prayer is something that I speak into wanting. A prayer for me. I pray angry. I pray weeping. I pray even with joy, to see my coworkers, we who travel at the edges of worlds. I thank God for every hospital worker in attendance. We few so close to death and dying who live in the pain of Friday and the longing of Saturday: I am thankful to serve in this huddle at the hospital, each of us a shaft of light in a storm that will not pass.

Because some storms do not. Sometimes Sunday does not come. Some storms stay. But some people—they stay too. Each of us has stayed. My chaplain supervisor would tell me to look for these kinds of moments, light seeping, life moving in. In chaos, this is resurrection. It is a hope for the true story of the world. A rumor. A rumor of staying. It is a preview of where we are going. Futures, every future, may end in a box. But I hope, even against absurdity, in open tombs, unburials, ex-caskets, the upturned soil of a sun-drenched grave. Is it true? I wish I knew. I hope so. I hope the rumor is true.

Baby girl. In the stars. I knew you. I know you. I will know you.

After the service, I share the news with my fellow chaplains who are working that day. And they weep with me. Hold me, weep, no words. Only witness.

There in the faces of my fellow chaplains as they share my wound, in each of them I am looking into the face of God, and they give me this:

*Each of them is my Sunday, holding me through Friday,*
*and their presence is a hint of promise.*
*My dream is gone, yet still with them, I will dream.*

*I've only dreamed of John once.*

*I'm in his hospital room. Machines, tubes, gown. Rise and fall of his chest, like a slow bubble forming, then pop. I am watching him die again.*

*And John suddenly sits up. Removes the ventilator. Removes his IV. Puts two feet on the floor. Fixes his gown. Looks at me. He smiles that funny, sheepish grin. Then walks out the door.*

*I follow him. He is headed to the exit. His walk is slow, deliberate, not his usual fast stride. I notice around us, there are dozens of patients walking to the exit, a current of people. I recognize them. I remember them.*

*There's Sammy. She had died on the operating table. Her sister, Sunny, had gotten to talk with her moments before the surgery. "I love you," they had said to each other over and over. It was all there was left to say. That was their last conversation. When Sunny had been told her sister died, she had fallen over in the waiting room, slamming the floor, wailing. I remember what I had told her. "Your sister knows. She knows you loved her." Sunny had looked at me, wailing, saying over and over, "She knows. She knows."*

*There's Mr. Hong. MSOF, multiple system organ failure. His wife, Mrs. Hong, had said goodbye to him in Korean as he was extubated. I had understood every word. "Thank you for marrying me. I don't want you to hurt anymore. Be good. I will live well." Mr. Hong sees me now. Touches my shoulder. Nods and makes a Korean noise, the affirmative grunt, "응.그래." Eung. Geurae.*

*Henry. He had challenged me to a push-up contest. "It's all I can do in here, my push-ups." He jumps up. He does seventy-five on the floor, right in front of me. "Brain tumor got nothing on chest day," he says. He dies three weeks later. Henry sees me walking. Thumps my chest. Laughs.*

*Norma. She's a ninety-something-year-old patient who requested a*

199

*final prayer. We held hands and she cried loudly, "I want my mommy. I want my mom." She tells me how much she had missed her mom all these years. These are some of her last words. She sees me, a glint in her eye. "She's calling me home. I hear her. I can hear her."*

*Jeremy. He was a teen who told me he didn't want to die and asked me to baptize him. I see Lanisha, a baby who made it to twenty-six weeks, being held by another patient, Miriam, who had a heart attack at her birthday dinner with her two daughters and died during resuscitation. José, who was telling jokes at the start of my shift, but had died by the end of my shift. Freyda, who had just graduated college but was struck in a hit-and-run driving home, was given a thoracotomy in the trauma bay so the physician could massage her heart to revive her. She regained a pulse but she never woke up. Carlos, who extended his life by six years with a heart transplant and had reconciled with his son, six years together; he never made it out from the third Code Blue. He is holding the hand of a child, Madison, who died of a brain injury from abuse. I see Kemel, who cried and cried over his gastric cancer, always in pain, always with music on, and he sees me and does a quick dance. There is Bravo Doe, the patient we couldn't identify, both of his thumbs up. Then one of my first patients, Lonnie, who had been kicked out by his mother and then overdosed alone, who tells me, "Thank you for looking after Mom."*

*I think I see Mayzie, with his parents, and Mayzie is walking full long steps, that big smile of his from ear to ear. I've missed him, his face, his voice, the way he lit up a whole room with just a look.*

*My patients. They see me. Some of them talk to me. Some smile. Wave. Nod. We are all walking off the floor. And I want to go. I want to go where they're going.*

*I'm not sure when it happens, but all of my patients, dozens, maybe hundreds of them, switch from their gowns to their clothes. I see scars fall. Stitches float. Lacerations close. Cancer lift out, dissolve.*

*My patients. I remember them. Every one of them. They are part of me. And in every way that I knew how, I loved them. I cannot, will not, let them go. I will never get over them. I'm not sure I want to.*

*I'm next to John. He is in a dress shirt, jeans, his hair in place, his face as bright as the day I met him.*

*I have to think of something. The things I didn't get to say.*

*We walk off the floor. But instead of the hallway to the elevators, there's a wall straight ahead. Everyone is walking to the wall. Then through the wall. One by one, disappearing.*

*I am trying to understand.*

*Then it is John's turn. He turns to me.*

*I tell him, "John. I—I wish I had something to say to you. I just. I miss seeing you. I'm sorry. I should've—I don't know. I'm sorry. I could've done something."*

*John grins that grin. Puts a hand on my shoulder.*

*He says to me, "It's okay. It's okay. I'm okay."*

*"John. It's hard without you here. It's really hard."*

*He gives a light squeeze.*

*I tell him, "John. You go. I go. If you go, I go."*

*"No," he says to me. "The other way. Where you go, I'll go."*

*I nod. I understand.*

*He turns to the wall. He walks through.*

*I wake up. I wake up with his words. Where you go, I'll go.*

*I say out loud, "Goodbye, John. Thank you. Thank you for being my friend."*

In my work, I have heard thousands of lives. I've lived them all, in some way. By hearing, I see. At times I feel lucky to be let in. To know so many. Other times I am bursting at the edges with the anguish of the irreversible. I do not want to forget their names, their laughter, their memories. To forget feels disloyal. I must honor their tears, to always hold them near.

"My world has stopped," a widow tells me, "and I want everybody to stop with me. But the world keeps going."

I try to stop the world for them. All I can do is try.

Stop the world, even briefly, to tell the story. Scream the story. Speak our grief.

I am a microphone for this grief, a death protested. I will hear a thousand lifetimes, if it means to keep the lost alive.

I need to tell you, if you have never heard it before:

*It is worth stopping the world to remember them.*

I have said before that I am a grief catcher. The bereaved are falling. Into a vacuum, into overwhelm, into a "new normal," falling on the floor. I try to catch them. Not to stop their grief, but to be with them on the way down.

Before reentering the hectic rush of living, back to city speed, back to the unrelenting tempo of numbers and institutional gears, we pause. I pause. So many need permission to let loose the river of all they are holding in this moment. In some small way, if I can give that permission, I will.

# EVERY WOUND IS A CALLING

"때는 두 번 이르지 아니하고 일은 지나면
못하나니 속히 분발할지어다."
*"For the time does not come twice,*
*and the work cannot pass,*
*so let our work run fast."*

— EXCERPT FROM THE KOREAN INDEPENDENCE WOMEN'S
DECLARATION OF THE MARCH 1ST MOVEMENT IN 1919,
AS RECITED BY ACTIVISTS SUCH AS YU GWAN-SUN

On the television, war is raging.

My patient Darius notices. He pauses midsentence, stares at horrors.

It is not his grief, it is not mine. But it is ours. Every second, another loss to grieve.

Through a screen by the ceiling, the pain of the world feels distant. But we know it's not far. Not far enough.

In the hallway, I hear concentrated echoes of screaming, patients in need. Just outside these walls, down alleys, across the ocean, I know there are more. On the television, I see a death toll. In the hospital, a life toll.

A physician gives an update to a family member in the waiting room. But that family member is distracted by the television there. Another shooting. Another explosion. Another racist attack. He barely hears the doctor. He is already bombarded.

Some grief, we know we are meant to grieve. But this traumatic grief, our collective rage? How do we triage a world in emergency?

A patient, a headline, a nation: It's all unbearable.

I am that person who reads the news and weeps. I want to reach into these headlines and sew up every wound with my bare hands. Every dollar I keep is too much for me; where can I give it all away? How can I see the world and be still another day?

I remember my two-year-old daughter's question, asked repeatedly after my wife's miscarriage: "How come baby gone?" I had answered her every time, in different ways. Trying to protect her from the harshness of an unfair world. But she kept asking: "How come?" And I ran out of answers. I was, in the end, only able to hold her.

My daughter, really, was looking for more than a reason. She was looking to my face. Seeking landing. For her lamenting. For her pain and her questions. I could fix her broken toy, bandage a gash. This? I could only try to be a warm place where she needed no shoes and all her lament was welcome. It is welcome.

My patient Darius looks back at me and says, "I don't understand. I don't get how we're still fighting. I don't understand how we're still so mad. I'm hurting every second, and I see the news, and people still want to hurt each other. The things we could do, you know, and we choose this instead."

He tells me he's angry. He asks me to pray. For him. For the world. For his cancer to heal. For the world to resolve. This prayer, in his condition, is his only protest.

A prayer. *May we seek the face of God in our neighbor. May we move in our lanes given. May our bodies find healing in every way they can. May our hands be for reaching, to build gardens, not walls. We cannot do it all, but first we listen. We get rest in, and we press in.*

I consider these words from the poem "Think of Others" by the late Mahmoud Darwish:

> *As you think of others far away, think of yourself*
> *(say: "If only I were a candle in the dark").*[1]

Across the ocean or at our front door, every wound is a calling. We must tend to the wound. It is overwhelming, to consider where to start. One stitch, one suture, will this be enough?

I only know that at the foot of this hospital bed, I seek the face of God in my patient. And in my patient's face, the face of God is seen.

In a world of horrors, what is holy is continuing to seek the sacred in another. I see you. Name your pain. Validate your wound. Call forth all you need, as long as you need, to grieve angry and to pursue repair.

If you needed permission, here it is.

Do not hide your tears. They are yours. In some measure, they are ours.

# ACKNOWLEDGMENTS

I have said before that I am not self-made, but We Made. I really mean that. There are so many to thank and I will miss someone. A good problem, I think.

Thank you: To Juliette, my wife. To A., my daughter. To my future son. My free time is family time because together we're free. I was always scared to have a family. When I dreamed of having one, you are the one I'd dream of. You know what I always say: *I love you. Please don't forget.*

Thank you: To my brother, Hoon. My parents, in-laws, siblings-in-law, to Rosco, to my cousins. You still get excited to watch my interviews. You keep my feet on the ground, you keep me excited for this work.

My coworkers: I'm not the chaplain I am today without you. They say that we plant seeds so the ones after us can sit in the shade of the tree. I am lucky to sit in your shadow. Thank you to Jenny, Waleska, Phyllis, Alisha, Sam, Laura, Amy, and Larry, whom I have mentioned in this book. Thank you to Kevin for praying for me through the writing. To each and every chaplain and healthcare worker (social workers and nurses, a special shout-out), I am forever grateful to you. Thank you to the amazing hospital staff: I am lucky to work with those who are world-class in every way.

Thank you to the wonderful team at W Publishing. To my editor, Lisa-Jo: I have loved working with you on this book, our very lively conversations with a lot of hand movements, and I am thankful for you giving me life on some very hard days. You are, really, a gift. Thank you to my incredible agent, Andrea, and to the team at The Bindery Agency for believing in me and receiving all of me. Thank you to K.J. for your love and care in connecting me with The Bindery.

Thank you to Rev. Beth Bostrom and Ji-Youn Kim for supporting me in test-reading several chapters. Your feedback made this book better, made me better. Thank you to Dr. Anita, who rooted for me the entire way through the loneliness of writing.

Thank you: Austin, Jacob, Andre, for cheering me on from day one. You've seen everything and you stayed. Mark, grateful for our friendship as we continually honor your brother John. Rob, thank you; you supported me so early on. Manny, Darren, Daryl, Stacey, Beth O., David, Patrick, Tommy, and HL: Each of you has cheered me on. To my therapist, Sheryle, thank you for lifting me to land. Thank you always to Kyle and Michelle R., who connected me with my very first agent.

To every educator and therapist and activist I've met online: I am always starstruck that you'd dialogue with me and I am in awe of your voices. The world is better with you here in it.

Thank you to my patients. You are the heroes, the champions of your story. I am glad to be a cameo. I changed many details to keep you secret, but your hearts and stories are kept alive in these pages.

To Creator and Creative God, the Christ of the Gospels: Thank you. For grace. I recall the words of a Jewish chaplain who told me that a rabbi would in one pocket carry a slip of paper that says, *I am but dust and ashes,* and in the other pocket another slip that says, *But for my sake, the world was created.* I ponder this mystery. I know too intimately what it is to return to dust. You love me, dust. You hold stars, and somehow you hold me.

# NOTES

## INTRODUCTION

1. A paraphrase from *It's OK That You're Not OK: Meeting Grief and Loss in a Culture That Doesn't Understand*, by Megan Devine (Boulder, CO: Sounds True, 2017), 169. Her original quote is, "There is no moving on. There is only moving with: an integration of all that has come before, and all you have been asked to live."
2. The authoritative manual of diagnosis in psychology, as defined by the American Psychiatric Association (APA). The most updated *DSM* as of this writing is the fifth and a half iteration, the *DSM-5-TR*, released in 2022.
3. Ellen Barry, "How Long Should It Take to Grieve? Psychiatry Has Come Up With an Answer," *New York Times*, March 18, 2022, https://www.nytimes.com/2022/03/18/health/prolonged-grief-disorder.html.

## CHAPTER 1: LOSS OF FUTURE DREAMS: A SKIP IN TIME

1. Theresa Hak Kyung Cha, *Dictee* (Oakland: University of California Press, 2022), 38.
2. Ted Chiang, *Exhalation* (New York: Knopf, 2019), 270–338.
3. Zora Neale Hurston, *Dust Tracks on a Road* (New York: Harper Perennial, 1996), 176.
4. Oliver Sacks, "A Matter of Identity," in *The Man Who Mistook His Wife for a Hat* (New York: Touchstone, 1998), 108–15.

5. I first heard this concept from author and speaker Jo Saxton in a talk she gave in 2019. She told the story of when she ignored her chest pain for three days and ended up in the hospital. She asked us the question, "If your heart could speak, what would it say?"

## CHAPTER 2: LOSS OF FAITH: A HOLE-SHAPED GOD

1. C.S. Lewis, *A Grief Observed* (New York: HarperCollins, 1994), 6–7.
2. Much more on this in chapter 6: Loss of Humanity.
3. Lewis, *A Grief Observed*, 28.

## CHAPTER 3: LOSS OF MENTAL HEALTH: ALL WE COULD HAVE DONE

1. South Korea has one of the highest national suicide rates in the world, with some estimates as high as 142.7 out of 100,000 people (compared to 14.2 out of 100,000 people in the US). In 2019 alone, more than 13,700 South Koreans took their own lives (out of 52 million people). There have been various local and national programs to prevent suicide, such as an emergency river-rescue team, the CARE program, encouraging audio messages and inscriptions along Han River, and AI to track those who may possibly jump from the Han River's bridges. Some of these programs, especially the messages along Han River, have been met with mixed response.

   Yoon Min-sik, "The Uphill Battle to Stop Han River Suicides," *Korea Herald*, December 31, 2022, https://www.koreaherald.com /view.php?ud=20221231000044.

   Minjae Choi, Yo Han Lee, "Regional Variation of Suicide Mortality in South Korea," *International Journal of Environmental Research and Public Health* 17, no. 15 (July 2020): 5433.

2. One in five US adults is diagnosed with mental illness. One in twenty is diagnosed with a severe mental illness. Over half of the US population will be diagnosed with a mental illness at some point in their lifetime.

   "Mental Health By the Numbers," *National Alliance on Mental Health Illness*, last updated April 2023, https://www.nami.org/mhstats.

"Mental Health: About Mental Health," *Centers for Disease Control and Prevention*, last updated April 2023, https://www.cdc.gov /mentalhealth/learn/index.htm.

3. Andrew Solomon, *The Noonday Demon: An Atlas of Depression* (New York: Touchstone, 2002), 69.

4. The Baker Act is a Florida statute and is a debatable form of "involuntary commitment." It has become common enough that other states have used the phrase "Baker Acted." In fiscal year 2020–2021, over thirty-eight thousand minors were involuntarily committed under the Baker Act in Florida, over a hundred per day, many of whom were taken in handcuffs.

Donna St. George, "In Florida, Showing Mental Health Struggles Could Get a Child dDtained," *Washington Post*, March 16, 2023, https:// www.washingtonpost.com/education/2023/03/16/florida-law-child -mental-health.

5. By now, some detailed research has been done on the link between social media usage and depression. Two meta-analyses (N = 244,676 and N = 451,229, respectively) show it is not necessarily about the social media usage itself, but "problematic" usage, which includes "negative quality" content and compulsive behaviors in viewing social media.

Chiungjung Huang, "A Meta-Analysis of the Problematic Social Media Use and Mental Health," *International Journal of Social Psychiatry* 68, no. 1 (December 2020): 12–33.

Simone Cunningham, Chloe C. Hudson, and Kate Harkness, "Social Media and Depression Symptoms: a Meta-Analysis," *Research on Child and Adolescent Psychopathology* 49 (January 2021): 241–53.

6. Claudia Carmassi et al., "Mania Following Bereavement: State of the Art and Clinical Evidence," *Front Psychiatry* 11 (May 2020): 366.

Several studies also show that suicide is possibly contagious. It is a phenomenon called *suicide contagion*.

"Suicide Prevention: Risk and Protective Factors," *Centers for Disease Control and Prevention*, last updated November 2, 2022, https://www.cdc.gov/suicide/factors/index.html.

Jamie Ducharme, "Suicide Deaths Are Often 'Contagious.' This

May Help Explain Why," *Time*, April 18, 2019, https://time.com/557 2394/suicide-contagion-study.

7. Pathologizing grief and mental illness, especially using the word *mania*, is a troubling aspect of diagnosing mental health. Grief should not qualify as mental illness, and the term *mental illness* itself is overly and broadly applied in many cases where a person's expressions or symptoms must be normalized.

8. On intergenerational safety nets composed of extended families pooling their resources: "Perhaps Australia and other countries could begin depression-proofing its economy by introducing extended family property ownership laws and incentives—as a bonus, this might also ease the welfare burden and decrease unemployment. If we're uncertain what such a model might look like, we might employ consultants from Australia's Asian community, which seems to be already operating an informal economy based on extended family models. Or we could just ask one of my grannies."

   Tyson Yunkaporta, *Sand Talk: How Indigenous Thinking Can Save the World* (New York: HarperOne, 2020), 44.

9. Angus Chen, "For Centuries, A Small Town Has Embraced Strangers With Mental Illness," *NPR*, July 1, 2016, https://www.npr.org/sections /health-shots/2016/07/01/484083305/for-centuries-a-small-town-has -embraced-strangers-with-mental-illness..

10. 1 Corinthians 12:26.

## CHAPTER 4: LOSS OF WORTH: WHAT YOU DESERVE

1. Judith L. Herman, *Trauma and Recovery: The Aftermath of Violence— From Domestic Abuse to Political Terror* (New York: Basic Books, 2022), 274.

2. Every year, the hospital where I'm a chaplain hosts a Child Abuse Prevention Symposium. In the rose garden outside there are pinwheels, flowers made of foil that spin in the wind, planted for every child whose life was saved by their medical team. In the fall of 2022, eighty-nine pinwheels were planted for abused children saved. Four balloons were also set in the garden, for the four children who

did not survive. In a two-year span, in West Central Florida alone, there were about seven thousand cases of child abuse reported to the Florida Abuse Hotline. Hillsborough County, where my hospital is located, ranks second in the state for child fatalities called in to the hotline.

"Tampa General Hospital to Host Child Abuse Prevention Symposium to Raise Awareness and Combat the Cycle of Violence," *Tampa General Hospital*, April 6, 2021, https://www.tgh.org/news/tgh -press-releases/2021/april/tampa-general-hospital-to-host-child-abuse -prevention-symposium-to-raise-awareness-and-combat-the.

3. For more context, Dr. Herman explains, "It is very tempting to take the side of the perpetrator. All the perpetrator asks is that the bystander do nothing. He appeals to the universal desire to see, hear, and speak no evil. The victim, on the contrary, asks the bystander to share the burden of pain. The victim demands action, engagement, and remembering. . . . To hold traumatic reality in consciousness requires a social context that affirms and protects the victim and that joins victim and witness in a common alliance. For the individual victim, this social context is created by relationships with friends, lovers, and family. For the larger society, the social context is created by political movements that give voice to the disempowered." Judith L. Herman, *Trauma and Recovery: The Aftermath of Violence—From Domestic Abuse to Political Terror* (New York: Basic Books, 2022), 10, 12.

4. Barry Lopez, *Crow and Weasel* (New York: Sunburst, 1998), 60.

5. This definition is a combination of several that I've heard through the years. The first time it was defined for me was by Dr. Jennifer McCain, neuropsychologist, who taught our didactic on trauma theory in the summer of 2017. Trauma was also defined for me by *The Deepest Well* by Dr. Nadine Burke Harris, and the Sanctuary Model developed by Dr. Sandra Bloom and her colleagues in the 1980s.

6. See the research of Dr. Rachel Yehuda. For more on the topic of trauma: Nadine Burke Harris, *The Deepest Well: Healing the Long-Term Effects of Childhood Trauma and Adversity* (Boston: Houghton Mifflin Harcourt, 2018).

On complex PTSD: Stephanie Foo, *What My Bones Know: A Memoir of Healing from Complex Trauma* (New York: Ballantine Books, 2022).

On racialized trauma: Resmaa Menakem, *My Grandmother's Hands: Racialized Trauma and the Pathway to Mending Our Hearts and Bodies* (Las Vegas: Central Recovery Press, 2017).

On systemic and intergenerational trauma: Natalie Y. Gutiérrez, *The Pain We Carry: Healing from Complex PTSD for People of Color* (Oakland: New Harbinger Publications, 2022).

7. For a primer on ACEs, see "Violence Prevention: Adverse Childhood Experiences (ACEs)," *Centers for Disease Control and Prevention*, updated June 29, 2023, https://www.cdc.gov/violenceprevention/aces/index.html.

The ACE score effectively predicts how childhood trauma affects physical and mental health, so that a score of four or more, for example, can increase risk of depression by almost 500 percent and risk of suicide over 1,000 percent.

Shaoyong Su et al., "The Role of Adverse Childhood Experiences in Cardiovascular Disease Risk: A Review with Emphasis on Plausible Mechanisms," *Current Cardiology Reports* 17, no. 10 (October 2015).

8. More on this in chapter 6. I dive into the difference between entitled anger and empathic anger.

Layla F. Saad (@laylafsaad), "When I first started out on my journey as an antiracist changemaker, the first thing I came upon is rage. My rage," Instagram photo, February 19, 2023, https://www.instagram.com/p/Co2dKdyITi8.

## CHAPTER 5: LOSS OF AUTONOMY: MOST OF ALL YOUR SELF

1. Persius, Satire 1, line 7.

2. Audre Lorde, *The Cancer Journals* (New York: Penguin Books, 2020), 41.

3. "'Disability justice' is a term coined by the Black, brown, queer, and trans members of the original Disability Justice Collective, founded in 2005 by Patty Berne, Mia Mingus, Stacey Milbern, Leroy Moore, Eli Clare, and Sebastian Margaret. Disabled queer and trans Black, Asian, and white activists and artists, they dreamed up a movement-building framework that would center the lives, needs, and organizing

strategies of disabled queer and trans and/or Black and brown people marginalized from mainstream disability rights organizing's white-dominated, single-issue focus." Leah Lakshmi Piepzna-Samarasinha, *Care Work: Dreaming Disability Justice* (Vancouver: Arsenal Pulp Press, 2018), 15.

4. Alice Wong, *Year of the Tiger: An Activist's Life* (New York: Vintage Books, 2022), 61.

5. Meghan O'Rourke, *The Invisible Kingdom: Reimagining Chronic Illness* (New York: Riverhead Books, 2022), 7.

6. Nicole Chung, *A Living Remedy: A Memoir* (New York: Ecco, 2023), 79.

## CHAPTER 6: LOSS OF HUMANITY: GRIEF, RAGE, AND THE UNMADE

1. W.E.B. Du Bois, *Black Reconstruction in America* (New York: Free Press, 1998), 714.

2. Michel Martin, "Slave Bible From The 1800s Omitted Key Passages That Could Incite Rebellion," NPR, December 9, 2018, https://www.npr.org/2018/12/09/674995075/slave-bible-from-the-1800s-omitted-key-passages-that-could-incite-rebellion.

3. This description is offered by Suh Nam-Dong, one of the pioneers of minjung theology, as quoted by researcher Jin-Ho Kim in his essay "*Ochlos* and the Phenomenology of Wretchedness," as part of the collected writings *Reading Minjung Theology in the Twenty-First Century* (Eugene, OR: Pickwick Publications, 2013), 203. See also the concept of liget, the "high voltage" emotion described by the Ilongot people in the Philippines.

The term *minjung* refers to "the people," particularly those in Korea who were sociologically and politically oppressed. Minjung theology is an interpretation of Christianity that sees the gospel of Jesus as a liberation of those with whom he had identified during his ministry, namely the exploited and impoverished. The minjung movement grew popular in the 1960s to 1980s, and minjung theology also focuses on social issues such as gender equality, the reunification of North and South Korea, environmental justice, and the empowerment of the working class. I was first introduced to the concept of minjung theology by author and activist Danté Stewart.

4. Nancy Jooyoun Kim, *The Last Story of Mina Lee* (New York: Park Row Books, 2020), 49.

5. Racialized trauma, while becoming more understood in mental health circles, is still too often pathologized as symptomatic of "psychosis"-like conditions, rather than addressed in terms of the events that caused the trauma. Just as grief is still occasionally pathologized as a symptom of an "abnormal" condition, so too is trauma.

"The more years that passed, the clearer it became that suffering is tied to racialized trauma and systemic issues beyond my patients' control. Many would numb out the grief, rage, anxiety, and hurt they experienced daily from microaggressions, sexism, homophobia, transphobia, and ableism—depending on their intersectional identities. So much of how we define ourselves was learned from racist institutions. The mental health field wasn't doing enough to understand this, and was actually quicker to pathologize patients like mine—for example, referring to deep fears as paranoid or delusional." Gutierrez, *The Pain We Carry*, 6–7.

6. Ellis P. Monk Jr., "Linked fate and mental health among African Americans," *Social Science & Medicine* 266 (September 2020).

Orla T. Muldoon et al., "Personal and Political: Post-Traumatic Stress Through the Lens of Social Identity, Power, and Politics," *Political Psychology* 42, no. 3 (December 2020): 501–33.

Grace Newton, "The Trauma and Healing of Consciousness," *Child Abuse & Neglect* 130, part 2 (August 2022).

Excerpt of study by Grace Newton: "I use the term trauma of consciousness to describe the trauma of simply knowing that violent, oppressive, and exploitive acts have happened in history and are currently happening to people with whom one shares an identity. The trauma of consciousness can encompass historical, intergenerational, or collective trauma but also expands recognition of trauma to people whose impacted identity is not one that passes through generations biologically. The trauma of consciousness can happen as a discreet event and may create a sense of collectivity among people who share a similar experience but do not necessarily live in a community where a continual story of trauma is told. Thus, individuals must seek out those with the shared identity . . . I believe this concept can apply to other marginalized groups including survivors of violence, LGBTQ people, disabled people, as well as domestic adoptees."

7. John E. Snyder et al., "Black Representation in the Primary Care Physician Workforce and Its Association with Population Life Expectancy and Mortality Rates in the US," *JAMA Network Open* 6, no. 4 (April 2023).

Another study suggests that "black doctors could reduce the black-white male gap in cardiovascular mortality by 19 percent." The data concludes that Black patients with Black doctors "increased their demand for preventives, particularly those which were invasive . . ." and ". . . brought up more issues and were more likely to seek advice from black doctors, as reflected in the doctors' notes."

Marcella Alsan et al., "Does Diversity Matter for Health? Experimental Evidence from Oakland," *American Economic Review* 109, no. 12 (December 2019).

Yet another study suggests that LGBTQ+ patients with an "LGBTQ+ affirming health care provider were more likely to seek preventative care, including routine checkups, colorectal screenings, flu shots, and HIV tests. Respondents with an LGBTQ+ affirming health care provider also reported higher control over their mental health and lower levels of cognitive decline. Overall, this study suggests that increasing access to LGBTQ+ affirming care could reduce health disparities among aging LGBTQ+ populations."

Harry Barbee et al., "Promoting Healthy Aging through LGBTQ+ Affirming Care," *Innovation in Aging* 6, no. S1 (December 2022): 44.

8. Resmaa Menakem, *My Grandmother's Hands: Racialized Trauma and the Pathway to Mending Our Hearts and Bodies* (Las Vegas: Central Recovery Press, 2017), 10.

9. Hilton Als, "Toni Morrison and the Ghosts in the House," *New Yorker*, October 19, 2003, https://www.newyorker.com/magazine/2003/10/27/ghosts-in-the-house.

Toni Morrison, in this interview, was responding to the title of Ralph Ellison's book *Invisible Man*. Morrison and Ellison had conflicting ideas on how to write about race. Though I lean toward Morrison's take—we are *silenced* when we've been falsely told we are silent—I certainly empathize with Ellison's feelings of invisibility.

10. Scott Bowles, "A Death Robbed of Dignity Mobilizes a Community," *Washington Post*, December 10, 1995, https://www.washingtonpost .com/archive/local/1995/12/10/a-death-robbed-of-dignity-mobilizes-a -community/2ca40566–9d67–47a2–80f2-e5756b2753a6/.

11. Maya Angelou, "Interview with Maya Angelou," @jenniferpagewriter, posted January 29, 2012, 5:14–5:35, YouTube video, https://www .youtube.com/watch?v=hSY7PokqMXk.

12. From the documentary *James Baldwin: The Price of the Ticket*, August 14, 1989, American Masters, https://www.pbs.org/wnet/americanmasters /james-baldwin-film-james-baldwin-the-price-of-the-ticket/2632.

13. Howard Thurman, *Jesus and the Disinherited* (Boston: Beacon Press, 2022), 3.

## CHAPTER 7: LOSS OF CONNECTION: LIFTING IN MIST, WE DRIFT

1. As noted in the introduction, the *DSM* is the *Diagnostic and Statistical Manual of Mental Disorders*, the authoritative manual of diagnosis in psychology as defined by the American Psychiatric Association (APA).

2. One out of ten American evangelicals left their church after the presidential election in 2016, because they disagreed with their church leaders' increasingly radicalized views. The other nine out of ten evangelicals who stayed had varying levels of disagreement, but chose not to leave.

Paul A. Djupe, Jacob R. Neiheisel, and Anand Edward Sokhey, "How Fights Over Trump Have Led Evangelicals to Leave Their Churches," *Washington Post*, April 11, 2017, https://www.washingtonpost .com/news/monkey-cage/wp/2017/04/11/yes-many-voters-left-their -congregations-over-trump-so-what-else-is-new.

3. In June of 2020, 60 percent of over eleven hundred adults considered George Floyd's death a murder. In March of 2021, nine months

later, this number dropped to 36 percent of over eleven hundred adults.

Susan Page, Sarah Elbeshbishi, and Mabinty Quarshie, "Exclusive: Stark Divide on Race, Policing Emerges Since George Floyd's Death, USA TODAY/Ipsos Poll shows," *USA Today*, March 5, 2021, https://www.usatoday.com/story/news/politics/2021/03/05 /americans-trust-black-lives-matter-declines-usa-today-ipsos-poll /6903470002.

Conflicting opinions on the murder of Breonna Taylor:

Ariel Edwards-Levy, "Poll: 41% Of Voters Say Breonna Taylor Grand Jury Too Lenient On Police," HuffPost, October 2, 2020, https://www.huffpost.com/entry/breonna-taylor-poll_n_5f778dd4c5b 64cf6a250262d.

In a poll by the *Economist*, 77 percent of Democrats believed that the murderers of Ahmaud Arbery should be found guilty, while 33 percent of Republicans believed they should be found guilty.

"*The Economist*/YouGov Poll: Nov 20–23, 2021—1500 U.S. Adult Citizens," YouGov, 83–4, https://docs.cdn.yougov.com /3ppnqjpghh/econTabReport.pdf.

There continues to be debate about whether the shootings at the spa in Atlanta on March 16, 2021, were to be labeled as hate crimes or having any racial motivation, despite six of the victims being Asian women. The Cherokee County sheriff captain and D.A., some investigators, and certain politicians have been quoted as denying any racial motivation.

Bill Chappell and Dustin Jones, "'Enough Is Enough': Atlanta-Area Spa Shootings Spur Debate Over Hate Crime Label," NPR, March 18, 2021, https://www.npr.org/2021/03/18/978680316/atlanta-spa -shootings-expose-frustration-and-debate-over-hate-crime-label.

A *CBS News* poll showed that in response to the question, "What happened at the Capitol on Jan. 6, 2021?" out of over two thousand adults, 85 percent of Democrats answered "an insurrection," compared to 21 percent of Republicans.

Jennifer De Pinto, "A Look at How Americans Have Viewed the

Jan. 6 Capitol Attack—CBS News Poll Analysis," *CBS News,* June 9, 2022, https://www.cbsnews.com/news/january-6-capitol-attack-cbs-news-poll-analysis.

4. bell hooks, *All About Love: Love Song to the Nation* (New York: HarperCollins, 2018), 172.

5. Stanley Milgram in 1972 used this term as a way to describe people we see every day. Though we familiarize ourselves with their dress or habits or speech, we never have a word with them. This is common today online, where you can know an entire person's life without talking with them for years. The way I learned this term in chaplaincy is far different.

6. Michelle Ye Hee Lee and Julia Mio Inuma, "Rent-a-stranger: This Japanese Man Makes a Living Showing Up and Doing Nothing," *Washington Post,* March 19, 2022, https://www.washingtonpost.com/world/2022/03/19/japan-loneliness-rent.

7. Jessie Yeung, Yoonjun Seo, "South Korea's Middle Aged Men Are Dying 'Lonely Deaths,'" CNN, December 18, 2022, https://www.cnn.com/2022/12/18/asia/south-korea-godoksa-lonely-death-intl-hnk-dst/index.html.

8. In contrast to ACEs, adverse childhood experiences, there are seven early positive childhood experiences, or PCEs, that act as an emotional vaccine to ACEs. One of these positive experiences is "at least 2 nonparent adults who took genuine interest [in us]." I think these types of connections are just as crucial in adult life. Not just mentors or coaches or pastors, but the ones who take an interest in us, especially in crises or at critical turning points.

   Christina Bethell et al., "Positive Childhood Experiences and Adult Mental and Relational Health in a Statewide Sample: Associations Across Adverse Childhood Experiences Levels," *JAMA Pediatrics* 173, no. 11 (November 2019).

9. Martin Buber, *I and Thou* (New York: Scribner, 2023), 26.

10. Gregory Boyle, *The Whole Language: The Power of Extravagant Tenderness* (New York: Avid Reader Press, 2021), 196.

11. John 19:26–27.

12. 1 John 4:12.

## CHAPTER 8: LOSS OF LOVED ONES: YOU GO, I GO

1. From *The Grieving Brain* by Mary-Frances O'Connor: "So, the more they tried to avoid thinking about the person, the more they thought about them unintentionally during mind wandering. From this we see that while cognitive avoidance can be a strategy that bereaved people use to get relief from frequent, painful thoughts of loss, higher avoidance also goes along with a higher number of intrusive thoughts. Suppressing one's thoughts is, ironically, related to a rebound of those thoughts. We need to discover new strategies to help bereaved people manage their painful thoughts in the present moment, since avoidance does not help them" (New York: HarperOne, 2022), 183–84.

2. Heung is nearly the inverse of Han, the feeling of sorrowful rage mentioned in chapter 6. In fact, both Heung and Han are often intertwined, exemplified by protests in Korea that are accompanied by singing and dancing. For more: Iljoon Park, "Korean Social Emotions: *Han* (한 恨), *Heung* (흥 興), and *Jeong* (정 情)," in *Emotions in Korean Philosophy and Religion*, eds. Edward Y.J. Chung and Jea Sophia Oh (London: Palgrave Macmillan, 2022), 235–66.

3. Zephaniah 3:17.

4. Alix Spiigel, "Invisibilia: A Man Finds An Explosive Emotion Locked In A Word," *NPR*, Jun 1, 2017, https://www.npr.org/sections/health-shots/2017/06/01/529876861/an-anthropologist-discovers-the-terrible-emotion-locked-in-a-word..

5. Lee Min-young and Kim Kang-min. "Cleaning up after 'godoksa,' lonely deaths in Korea," *The Korean Times*, last updated May 16, 2022, https://www.koreatimes.co.kr/www/nation/2024/01/178_329115.html.

6. Carrie Fisher, *Surrender the Pink* (New York: Simon and Schuster, 1990), 280.

7. Mary-Frances O'Connor, *The Grieving Brain: The Surprising Science of How We Learn from Love and Loss* (New York: HarperOne, 2022), 97–101.

8. Nikhita Kini (@nikhitakini), "It took me 2 years to complete this reel. I couldn't get myself to shoot the part where the package came

to my place ON dad's birthday (coincidentally)–March 8th 2021," Instagram reel, June 19, 2022, https://www.instagram.com/reel /Ce_lrHxg2MO.

"Woman Turns Father's Shirts into Quilt to Keep His Memories Alive," *News18*, last updated July 2, 2022, https://www.news18.com /news/buzz/woman-turns-fathers-shirts-into-quilt-to-keep-his -memories-alive-5473207.html.

9. Retrorider (@retroridersg), "Every Chinese new year whenever I miss my late grandma, I would come to google map and she will be there," TikTok post, January 27, 2023, https://www.tiktok.com/@retroridersg /video/7193211760843705601.

Anna Maria Romero, "Grandson Searches for His Late Grandmother on Google Maps Whenever He Misses Her Every CNY, Says 'Miss You Grandma,'" *Independent Singapore*, February 6, 2023, https://theindependent.sg/grandson-searches-for-his-late-grandmother -on-google-maps-whenever-he-misses-her-every-cny-says-miss-you -grandma.

10. Joan Didion, *The Year of Magical Thinking* (New York: Vintage International, 2007), 37.

11. *The Prophet* (Knopf 1923), last accessed on January 25, 2024, https:// poets.org/poem/farewell-2.

## EPILOGUE

1. Mahmoud Darwish, *Almond Blossoms and Others*, poem title "Think of Others." Translated by Mohammad Shaheen. (Massachusetts: Interlink Books, 2009), 3.

# ABOUT THE AUTHOR

**J.S. Park** is a hospital chaplain, author, and online educator. For eight years he has been an interfaith chaplain at a thousand-plus-bed hospital that is designated a Level 1 Trauma Center. His role includes grief counseling; attending every death, every trauma and Code Blue; staff care; and supporting end-of-life care. He also served for three years as a chaplain at one of the largest nonprofit charities for the unhoused on the East Coast.

J.S. has an MDiv, completed in 2010, and a BA in Psychology. He also has a sixth-degree black belt in Tae Kwon Do. J.S. currently lives in Tampa, Florida, with his wife, a nurse practitioner; his three-year-old daughter; and their adopted dog. They are expecting another child, their son.